Effective financial planning for library and information services

Second Edition

Duncan McKay

Effective financial planning for library and information services

Second Edition

Duncan McKay

Europa Publications
Taylor & Francis Group plc

Second edition 2003

© Duncan McKay 2003

Published by Europa Publications Limited 2003
11 New Fetter Lane
London EC4P 4EE
United Kingdom

(A member of the Taylor & Francis Group)

ISBN 0 85142 464 3

Contents

Figures

Tables

About the author

Duncan J McKay was appointed as the Document Management Team Lead with ConocoPhillips (UK) Ltd. in Aberdeen, in September 2002, following the merger of Conoco Inc. and Phillips Petroleum Co. His group provides services to the Upstream Organisation of ConocoPhillips ranging from traditional library services to records management.

Having spent the first two years of his career in the Scottish academic sector, Duncan then spent twelve years within the oil exploration and production sector of the British National Oil Corporation and its successors, Britoil plc and British Petroleum plc, in Glasgow. Another short period in academe, as the Radzinowicz Librarian of Criminology at Cambridge, preceded a return to the oil industry in 1991 when he joined Amerada Hess Ltd. After seven years with AHL, in a number of roles, he joined Saga Petroleum (UK) Ltd. as Information Centre Manager. Following the sale of Saga Petroleum in 2000 he joined Conoco (UK) as an Information Services Specialist within the Finding (Exploration) Geodata Management Group.

He has always had interests in the application of financial management techniques within the Library and Information business and has lectured on the topic to a number of academic institutions and professional meetings.

Until recently Duncan was heavily involved in professional activities. Duncan is a past Treasurer of the Library Association Industrial Group (Scotland)

and was Assistant Hon Treasurer, and then Hon Treasurer of the Institute of Information Scientists from 1990 to 1999.

Dedication

The second edition of this Know How Guide is dedicated to Carol for her support and encouragement during the revision of the manuscript, and for still being there when needed.

Acknowledgements

I would like to thank all those professional colleagues with whom I have discussed financial management over many years. Thanks are also due to those members of the information profession who, over the years, have nominated and elected me as Honorary Treasurer to various posts that have provided practical financial management experience to our mutual benefit.

The forbearance of the editors is gratefully acknowledged.

Amerada Hess Ltd has given its approval for the continuing publication of the 1995 procedures defined in Appendix B, although these are no longer actually in operation.

Conoco UK Ltd has given its approval for the publication of this volume but I would stress that the views expressed are entirely my own and do not necessarily reflect the views of Conoco UK Ltd.

Preface to second edition

In the six years since the publication of the first edition of this Know How Guide little has fundamentally changed in financial management for the information professional, except that its importance has grown.

As pressures of business continue to affect all information functions it has become ever more important to be able to justify the costs involved in running any form of information function.

The growing significance of the increasing availability of electronic publications in addition to or in place of traditionally published materials means a growing emphasis on purchasing access to documents rather than purchasing physical documents themselves.

This is an issue that crosses the entire sphere of management issues in the information unit and for this reason I have included Chapter 5, which discusses the subject. In respect of the actual budget and financial management process it is in effect simply another line item or service to be reviewed in the overall scheme of things.

Apart from this access versus purchase issue there are few other changes in this edition of the Guide. The increase in length has permitted the publication of a few additional figures to illustrate points. The reference list has also grown as the profession continues to accept the necessity of "managing" its finances.

1. Introduction

Since the mid 1980s it has been essential for librarians and information managers to be financially aware although it has always been the case that a few managers in the field have realised the critical importance of the financial aspects of their operations.

Almost 25 years ago, Hewgill (1) stated the obvious, at an ASLIB one-day conference:

'Accountancy is no mystic, druidic activity but a means devised by practical people to express the use of resources in a common measure – money.' Whilst Alley and Cargill (2) said in 1982: 'Many librarians are resigned to a career of inept fiscal management.'

It was possible, 16 years ago, for Roberts (3a, b) to say:

'The practice of costing library and information operations and the principles and techniques available to support the economic management of library and information services are one of the weakest areas in the repertoire of library management.'

Although I strongly believe that in the years since these statements were made significant progress has been achieved in ensuring that librarians and information workers are aware of the importance of financial management, it is still, I consider, *an area of weakness for many.*

The growing awareness of the importance of financial management has been caused, in part, by the many external pressures impacting on the information profession since the early 1980s. All libraries have suffered from constraints on financial resources, whether in the form of staff freezes, reductions in or standstills on their resource budgets. Recent trends in the information business have included:

- the perception of declining resources
- the introduction of contracting out into all sectors of the information world, from the corporate information unit through to the public library
- the impact of market testing programmes
- the move towards cost centre based management of financial resources
- the need to ensure that money expended on information services is 'well spent', i.e. the need to be seen to be organisationally accountable, whether to the public or to the organisation
- perceived demands for improved levels of service
- an increasing emphasis on the development and establishment of performance indicators
- an increasing need to make inter- rather than intra-organisational comparisons
- the move from purchasing *ownership of* information to purchasing *access to* information.

These trends have further emphasised the need for members of the information profession to have a fuller understanding of the processes involved in financial management. They will find it more and more important to be in a position to apply financial management techniques in areas such as:

- cost control
- using resources in the best fashion
- justification of additional resourcing
- justification of existing resource provisions
- income generation.

Information professionals have, I believe, finally realised that they have a fundamental need, in the words of the Warner (4), to 'own their numbers'.

In this short guide it will not be possible to expand in depth on the many facets of financial management. I hope, however, that the guide provides a basic overview of the major areas involved: budgeting, costing and financial reporting and accounting. In addition a brief review of the potential use of spreadsheets is given, whilst the reference list and bibliography are intended to give pointers to some of the many readings from the ever-growing and substantive literature on financial management in the information unit. I should add that the term 'information unit' is used throughout the text to refer to any kind of information provider, whether structured as a unit, department, centre or division.

I hope that the reader will find confirmation that there is nothing in the financial management process that is beyond the skill of the information professional who can count, who has basic computer skills, allowing the use of spreadsheets, and who has the will to convince herself or himself of the need to understand that accountants are not the only professionals involved in the overall information unit finance process.

2. Budgeting

The *Oxford English Dictionary* (5) defines 'budget' as a noun:

'A statement of probable revenue and expenditure for the ensuing year, with financial proposals funded thereon, annually submitted by the Chancellor of the Exchequer, on behalf of the Ministry, for the approval of the House of Commons. Sometimes put for the condition of the national finances as disclosed in the ministerial statement. Hence applied to an analogous statement by the finance minister of any foreign country; also to a prospective estimate of receipts and expenditure or a financial scheme, of a public body'.

The Supplement to the *Dictionary* (6) defines the verb as follows: 'to draw up or prepare a budget'.

A more useful definition would be: '...a statement of allocated expenditure and/or revenue, under specific headings, for a chosen period'.

In most organisations it is expected that the budget is not negotiable during the period that it covers.

The simple definitions are applicable to the process of budgeting within library and information units.

McElroy (7) wrote: 'It is as much a part of professional librarianship to fight the library's corner in the resource allocation committee as it is to carry out a literature search".

Stoffle (8) considers that: 'budgeting (the justifying, allocating, raising and managing of library funds) is one of the two essential components in library management, the other being creativity'.

Since Koenig (9) was writing, 21 years ago, that: 'Your budget ... is the ... central planning document...', the overall budgeting process has become more complex. In most library and information units the budgeting process has expanded and now includes all the elements of strategic planning. The process has also evolved from the simple use of line-item budgets, based purely on previous experience and expenditure, to a much more formal planning process.

In library and information unit terms, the overall purpose of a simple budget is to provide an approved framework within which the information manager can operate. As such the budget is purely a financial plan. Talbot (10) defines a budget as the 'statement in monetary terms of the organisational intent concerning the library's programs and priorities'.

It is essential that all concerned with the information unit understand that the overall budget process is also the means of providing political and social interaction between the unit and its organisation and user communities.

The overall planning and budgeting process may be divided into three stages:

- development of objectives for information unit (planning)
- preparation of the budget (budgeting)

- monitoring of performance against budget (financial reporting and accounting, discussed in Chapter 4).

2.1 Planning

Planning should be the first stage in the financial and budgetary process. The final product of the planning process is the strategic plan. Preparation of the plan will require an examination of all aspects of the information unit's mandate in terms of its impact on the organisation.

The processes in the planning process include:

- clarification and agreement of the broad goals and objectives of the organisation
- determination of directions and priorities
- provision of framework for policy and decision-making
- assistance in the effective allocation of resources
- determination of critical issues and constraints.

Amongst the many benefits that derive from the strategic planning process the most significant in terms of the budget process are described by Corall (11) as the 'better financial prospects for the library, as annual budget bids and cases for special funding can be presented with a strategic perspective'.

Detailed discussion of the planning process is outside the terms of this volume and readers are referred to the extensive literature available. Much has been written on the strategic planning process both in general management literature and in specific works for the library and information profession. Corrall (11) provides a basic reference listing.

2.2 Budgeting basics

The fundamentals of a budget are that:

- it is prepared to cover a defined period
- it is approved in advance of the period to which it refers
- the data used in its preparation are documented for future reference
- qualitative, quantitative and fiscal information are all combined in the budget process
- it defines processes that are to be adopted in order to ensure that the organisation's goals are met.

Although there are many ways of defining and discussing the budget process it should be stressed that the 'bottom-line' in the budget process will be a request for funds which will be the same *figure* irrespective of the presentational methods involved.

In terms of terminology budgets may be variously described by their type and method of preparation.

Budgeting based on preparation methods
Ranging from Line-Item to Zero Based Budgeting, there are various ways in which budgets can be prepared and presented.

Budgeting based on type of expenditure
Operating, or revenue, budgets represent the routine day to day budgets which provide the authorisation for general expenditure.

Capital budgets represent funds for major, one-off, purchases for which special rules apply. In most cases these costs are not included in the annual operating budget at full cost in the period of purchasing, but will be provided for over the life of the purchase through provisions for depreciation.

Most information units will normally be concerned only with operating budgets. The organisation's finance department frequently handles capital budgeting.

Budgeting based on management input
Budgets may be directive or participatory:

* directive budgets will be imposed by the information manager's management team
* participatory budgets will require the information unit to undertake the preparation; it is this latter type with which this volume is concerned.

2.3 Budget preparation

Six different budget preparation methods have been recognised, and all have received considerable coverage in the literature. The methods, presented below in increasing level of complexity, are:

* Line-Item Budgeting
* Formula Budgeting
* Programme Budgeting
* Performance Budgeting
* Planning Programming Budgeting System
* Zero Based Budgeting

2.3.1 Line-Item Budgeting

Line-Item Budgeting is the simplest and most familiar form of budgeting used. At its most simplistic, where the department is managed as one component within, for instance, an administration group, the budget would simply comprise a request for a certain sum to be spent on the purchase of publications.

Where the information unit is considered to be, or treated as, a cost centre in its own right, the Line-Item Budget would contain elements for all aspects of direct expenditure together with elements for overheads charged by other functions. The Line-Item Budget is also, of course, the simplest to compile; the data relies heavily on previous years' expenditure that is often increased purely in an incremental fashion.

Figure 1 illustrates a complex Line-Item Budget for the expenses of the fictitious XYZ Company's Information Centre 2002 Budget Proposal.

The budget document comprises four columns.

Column A lists the various components of expenditure under headings: Employee costs, Departmental overhead costs, Business expenses and Allocated overheads. Employee costs include the direct costs of payroll together with fringe benefits, which would include pension costs and such areas as share scheme costs or other activities. In many organisations these figures would be calculated by the finance department concerned based on agreed staffing figures.

In order to convey an indication of the budget provision over time three columns of figures are likely

XYZ Company Limited   Information Centre   Budget preparation 2002

	A	B	C	D
		2000 Spend	2001 Budget	2002 Proposal
1	Description			
2				
3				
4	Employee Costs	10+4	10+4	9+5
5	Payroll Costs (Permanent Staff)	192000	200000	189000
6	Payroll Costs (Contract Staff)	76800	80000	99750
7	Fringe Benefits	78720	82000	86100
8	Overtime	9600	10000	10500
9	Company NIC	20544	21400	22470
10				
11	Total Employee Costs	377664	393400	407820
12				
13	Departmental Overhead Costs			
14				
15	Books and Monographs	28659	30000	31000
16	Journals	78654	82000	86000
17	Newspapers & Press Cuttings	19762	22000	25000
18	Online Services (call-off)	15643	25000	35000
19	Online Services (current awareness)	0	3500	5000
20	Scouting Services	23000	26000	27500
21	Maps	2450	2400	2500
22	Bibliographic & Indexing Tools	1987	2000	2100
23	Other Services			
24				
25	Total Publications	170155	192900	214100
26				
27	Data Storage Costs	295349	315000	310000
28	Computing Services Recharged	56000	58000	60000
29				
30	Total Departmental Overheads	521504	565900	584100
31				
32	Business Expenses			
33				
34	Professional Fees/consultants	0	4000	2500
35	Travel (Staff)	2500	2550	2700
36	Accommodation & Subsidence (Staff)	1300	1400	1500
37	Entertainment (Non-staff)	300	1000	1000
38	Staff Conferences	2856	3000	3000
39				
40	Total Business Expenses	6956	11950	10700
41				
42	Allocated Overheads - Office Space	60910.2	64116	68924.7
43	Allocated Overheads - Office Services	63612	66960	71982
44	Allocated Overheads - Personnel	10670.4	11232	12074.4
45	Allocated Overheads - Finance	1504.8	1584	1702.8
46				
47	Total Allocated Overheads	136697.4	143892	154683.9
48				
49	Total Cost Centre	1042821.4	1115142	1157303.9

Figure 1:   Complex line-item budget

11

to be presented. In column B the actual expenditure incurred during 2000 is shown. Column C lists the components for 2001, the current year, whilst column D gives the proposal for 2002 – the year for which the budget is being compiled.

The budget presented in Figure 1 is intended to be purely illustrative in nature, as all organisations will have their own methods for describing the budget.

In some organisations it is likely that the 'Total publications' line (line 25) would be the only line in the budget describing publications. For internal purposes the information unit would still require detailed analysis of the various types of publications to be purchased during the year.

In other organisations the information manager may need to be involved in the preparation of a budget which would include costs for office equipment and services used. In our example these would be included in the various 'Allocated overheads' headings.

Although Line-Item Budgets provide basic financial management for the information unit, they provide no information about how expenditure relates to the objectives and programmes of the department. Despite this potentially serious drawback, Line-Item Budgets will always be a significant part of the financial management process as all managers need to be aware of what is being spent on what.

2.3.2 Formula Budgeting

Formula Budgeting is a type of budget system which until the early 1990s was much more common in the

United States than the United Kingdom and Europe. Here the budget allocation is simply calculated by a formula such as:

- the number of students attending particular courses
- the number of faculty members
- the population of the local authority concerned with provision.

The formula may then be used to determine either absolute cash allocations or the percentage of the overall 'cake' that is allocated to each unit.

However, Lovecy (12) notes the need for university librarians to make use of 'book allocations' – effectively a type of formula budget. Lovecy cites internal Edinburgh University papers listing various factors from undergraduate student numbers to the cost of materials, which should be considered during calculation of the formulae for the allocation of the library's book fund to the departments that it will service.

2.3.3 Programme Budgeting

Programme Budgets are the stage beyond the simple Line-Item Budget. Within a Programme Budget the services and activities are emphasised rather than the direct costs themselves. Items of expenditure are allocated to the specific activities for which they will be used, for instance, reference services and loan services. The final product will be seen as an extension of the Line-Item Budget, see Figure 2. The figure shows that Programme Budgeting is an addition to the budget process, supplementing the Line-Item Budget rather than replacing it. This method of budgeting allows budget requests to be matched to the goals and plans of the information unit. Black (13) provides an overview of the process involved in converting from Line-Item to Programme Budgeting, noting that those institutions that do not use Programme Budgeting have, normally, not had the management or staff resources to do so.

XYZ Company Limited   Information Centre   Budget preparation 2002

2000 Spend	2001 Budget	Description	2002 Library Servic	Information Servi	Data Managemen	Total
10+4	10+4	Employee Costs	1+0.25	2+0.75	6+4	9+5
192000	200000	Payroll Costs (Permanent Staff)	21000	42000	126000	189000
76800	80000	Payroll Costs (Contract Staff)	4987	14963	79800	99750
78720	82000	Fringe Benefits	9566	19135	57399	86100
9600	10000	Overtime	1000	0	9500	10500
20544	21400	Company NIC	2497	4993	14980	22470
377664	393400	Total Employee Costs	39050	61091	287679	407820
		Departmental Overhead Costs				
28659	30000	Books and Monographs	31000			31000
78654	82000	Journals	79000	7000		86000
19762	22000	Newspapers & Press Cuttings	22500	2500		25000
15643	25000	Online Services (call-off)		35000		35000
0	3500	Online Services (current awareness)		5000		5000
23000	26000	Scouting Services		27500		27500
2450	2400	Maps	2500			2500
1987	2000	Bibliographic & Indexing Tools	2100			2100
170155	192900	Total Publications	137100	77000	0	214100
295349	315000	Data Storage Costs			310000	310000
56000	58000	Computing Services Recharged	8000		52000	60000
521504	565900	Total Departmental Overheads	145100	77000	362000	584100
		Business Expenses				
0	4000	Professional Fees/consultants	0	0	2500	2500
2500	2650	Travel (Staff)	0	500	2200	2700
1300	1400	Accommodation & Subsidence (Staff)	133.928571	294.6428571	1071.428571	1500
300	1000	Entertainment (Non-staff)	100	400	500	1000
2856	3000	Staff Conferences	267.857143	589.2857143	2142.857143	3000
6956	11050	Total Business Expenses	501.785714	1783.928571	8414.285714	10700
60910.2	64116	Allocated Overheads - Office Space	6153.99107	13538.78936	49231.92857	68924.7
63612	66960	Allocated Overheads - Office Services	6426.96429	14139.32143	51415.71429	71982
10670.4	11232	Allocated Overheads - Personnel	1078.07143	2371.757143	9624.571429	12074.4
1504.8	1584	Allocated Overheads - Finance	152.035714	334.4785714	1216.285714	1702.8
136697.4	143892	Total Allocated Overheads	13811.0625	30384.3375	110488.5	154683.9
1042821.4	1115142	Total Cost Centre	198462.848	190259.2661	768581.7857	1157303.9

Figure 2:   Illustrative Programme budget (Service Groups)

Figure 2 illustrates the principle and extends the data from Figure 1 to show a department with three major programmes of activities.

Columns A to C provide details of the year 2000 expenditure, the 2001 budget and budget components.

Columns D to F list the budget request for each of the programmes:

- library services – the development and maintenance of the basic collection of publications which provide the backbone of any information unit

- information services – the provision of all forms of information services ranging from current awareness to online information retrieval services

- data management services – the provision of administration and storage services for corporate hard copy data services.

Supporting information on the development of each of these programmes might take the following form.

Library services – continuing provision of a broad range of library purchasing services to all divisions of the company. The budget proposal includes allowances for inflation only with a few significant changes in budget as follows:

- Newspapers – increases in newspaper budget are intended to provide coverage in the HQ service of activities in region X together with the direct provision of English papers for region X's office that is due to open in April 2002.

- Information services – continuing provision of a broad range of information services to all divisions of the company.

- Data management services – to manage the archival data of the company with a long-term view of reducing cost in real terms. Reduced costs are expected in view of the significant process made in retention policy development.

Column G presents the total budgets for each line-item. Notice how the total budget is the same as in column D of Figure 1.

This example provides just one method of breaking down the overall expenditure of the information unit.

It would be just as possible to develop a programme budget in which the expenditure was broken down by the departments being served, for instance Exploration, Production, Marketing, Chemicals, Shipping. Figure 3 illustrates both this form of programme budgeting and also the way in which programme budgets can be used as summaries of the information unit's budget, where the headings reflect a consolidation of a lower level Line-Item Budget. The 'bottom line' in both examples will be seen to be the same (£1,157,304).

XYZ Company Limited   Information Centre   Budget preparation

2005 Spend	2001 Budget	Description	Exploration	Development	Marketing	Chemicals	Shipping	Total
10+4	10+4	Employee Costs	4+1.5	1+1.5	3+1	1+0.5	0+0.5	9+5
198300	200000	Payroll Costs (Permanent Staff)	84000		21000	68000	21000	0	116000
76800	80000	Payroll Costs (Contract Staff)	29600	30600	19600	10000	15000	98750
78720	82000	Fringe Benefits	38270	9566	28636	9566	0	86100
9800	10000	Overtime	6000	500	3500	600		118500
20544	21400	Company NIC	9785	2497	7591	2497		22470
377964	393400	Total Employee Costs	167554	64163	122536	43563	10000	407820
		Departmental Divisional Costs						
28656	30000	Books and Monographs	11000	18000	6000	2000	2000	31000
76654	80000	Journals	36000	38000	7000	3500	2500	86000
18702	22000	Newspapers & Press Cuttings	7900	7800	3300	3300	3300	25000
15643	26000	Online Services (call-off)	11000	10500	6000	2000	2000	32000
0	3500	Online Services (current awareness)	1500	500	2000	500	500	5000
27000	26000	Standing Services	27500					27500
2400	2400	Maps	2000	250	125	125		2500
1997	2000	Bibliographic & Indexing Tools	750	750	600			2100
170196	192000	Total Publications	100890	62100	25025	11425	10000	214100
291349	315000	Data Storage Costs	19000	129500	5000	2500	3000	315000
59000	58000	Computing Services Recharged	20500	20000	8000	6000	6000	50000
521504	565000	Total Departmental Overheads	310250	159600	35025	19925	19000	684100
		Business Expenses						
0	4000	Professional Fees/consultants	975	445	712.5	267.5	100	2500
2500	2500	Travel (Staff)	1054.4	480.6	776	290	95	2750
1300	1400	Accommodation & Subsistence (Staff)	588	267	427	163	55	1500
300	1000	Entertainment (Non-staff)	380	180	285	110	35	1000
2856	3000	Staff Conferences	1175	534	855	330	105	3000
6956	11900	Total Business Expenses	4187.4	1906.6	3055.5	1180.5	390	10750
60810.2	64115	Allocated Overheads - Office Space	27185	12200	19700	7375	2465	68924.7
6381.2	6090	Allocated Overheads - Office Services	28287	12800	20750	7675	2510	71982
10670.4	11232	Allocated Overheads - Personnel	4745	2155	3490	1294	430	12074.4
1504.8	1584	Allocated Overheads - Finance	650	290	509	170	60	1702.8
136697.4	143992	Total Allocated Overheads	80957	27446	44363	16514	5465	154603.9
1042921.4	1115142	Total Cost Centre	542899.4	290114.6	257972.5	81162.5	35155	1157303.9

Figure 3   Illustrative Program budget (Divisional Groups)

The literature of library and information science provides numerous examples of Programme Budgeting, of which the following are selected examples.

Robinson and Robinson (14) quote a costing survey in five public libraries in Monterey County, California, and define eight programmes:

- reference/client referral
- interlibrary loan/photocopying for ILL
- circulation/in-house use
- collection management

- public space
- library administration
- in-house programmes
- other programmes (a catch-all).

Stewart (15) shows an analysis of Gloucestershire's library that includes programmes for "Education and Leisure Services for Young Persons and Adults":

- academic and vocational education
- non-vocational study and cultural activity
- youth services
- recreation
- community activities.

Pearson and Yates-Mercer (16a, b) in their survey of charging in corporate information services presented a listing of services that could be charged for, all of which could be considered as programmes. These included:

- lending of publications
- journal circulation
- interlibrary loans
- photocopying services
- current awareness/SDI services
- information searches, both manual, online and CD-ROM
- production of evaluated reports.

Programme Budgeting will be seen to have significant advantages over the simple line-item version in that it provides linkages between the inputs to the information unit and the outputs from it. The technique forces a review of the services provided, whilst at the basic managerial level, proper implementation of a Programme Budget will permit the preparation of better and more convincing budgets.

2.3.4 Performance Budgeting

The Performance Budget depends on the calculation of costs for each individual activity undertaken by the information unit. Once these costs have been calculated then the budget is 'simply' established by multiplying the unit cost by the proposed level of activity.

These budgets do at first glance appear to be scientific but Koenig (9) draws attention to the major drawbacks:

- costing is a complicated activity (as will be seen in Chapter 3)
- the difficulty of explaining the complications of library operational management to library and information service management: for instance: 'Why does it cost ten pounds to circulate a document when you can buy another copy for nine pounds'?.

2.3.5 Planning Programming Budgeting System (PPBS)

The PPBS method has been the most widely implemented method of Programme Budgeting and has an extremely voluminous literature. PPBS is, however, one of the most complex methods of budgeting, incorporating many elements of long range planning techniques. The system, when fully operational, allows information managers to make better decisions on resource allocations by developing an overview of goals at the organisational level, rather than the information unit level.

The preparation of a PPBS budget will require:

- the establishment of the organisation's goals
- the selection of specific objectives from a variety of possible objectives which are of relevance to the goals of the organisation, not from the current processes – objectives should also not be restricted to those of the information unit alone
- the collection of data in order to determine appropriate objectives
- the selection of the most appropriate means of achieving the selected objectives
- the development in detail of the ways in which the objectives are to be achieved which should include a review of current procedures as well as an evaluation of new ideas
- the consequent determination of the budgets and organisational impact of the plan.

PPBS thus involves the whole gamut of strategic planning for the information unit. It is *essential* that goals should be established as far up the organisation as possible rather than at information unit level. Once objectives have been developed then the information manager can determine the possible means of achieving the defined goals following which the appropriate budgets can be established.

The final budget presentation will show the alternative methods, together with their costs, that are available to provide the specified services for the information unit. These presentations will allow management to decide how to achieve the goals of the information unit.

The final stages of the PPBS procedure will involve:

*   the development of measures that allow the achievement against objectives to be determined; PPBS requires measurable indicators so that performance can be measured against 'real' objectives

*   the implementation of the selected programmes

*   the measurement of performance

*   the evaluation of the programme's effectiveness against the standards defined during the budget development.

2.3.6 Zero Based Budgeting (ZBB)

Zero Based Budgeting is an extended variant of the PPBS system and when fully implemented assumes that each programme, or activity, within the information function is re-justified from a 'zero basis' for each budget year. In other systems, budgets have been seen as simply building on the previous year's budgetary submissions/allocations as in the Line-Item Budget. In a ZBB system, all parts of the organisation start with a nil budget and must build their submissions from that basis.

Throughout the ZBB process it is always assumed that even where an activity is worthwhile, and considered for continuation, it could be carried out for a lower cost than currently incurred. For example,

21

in the public library field it might be considered that the only role for village libraries is for circulation of documents – libraries could therefore be opened for very short but regular hours with all other services being provided by the central city library. A final point to be stressed is that where an activity cannot be justified in terms of the organisation's goals and objectives then that activity should be discontinued!

ZBB uses the term 'decision package' for what in Programme Budgeting would be termed cost centres or programmes.

Each decision package will:

- relate to a specific programme
- specify the operations to be undertaken;
- detail the benefits and impacts of the programme
- specify the costs involved
- provide details of the implications of providing the programme at varying levels, rather than simply on a go or no-go basis.

After the packages have been established and reviewed they will provide input into the overall management of the budget cycle, which will allow for the determination of the use and allocation of the organisation's resources.

ZBB has the same benefits as PPBS in that the process:

- requires planning before budget preparation
- provides budgets that are tied to the goals of the organisation

- ensures that management information is much improved
- enables staff at all levels to be more closely involved.

One can see that both ZBB and PPBS require the objectives of the organisational unit to be established before the budgetary resources are examined. They are methods of ensuring a strategic planning attitude is adopted within the information unit. However, although ZBB and PPBS are seen as effective methods of ensuring that the budgetary process is managed effectively, they can be exceedingly formal. Both methods fell into some disuse in the library and information field during the 1970s when they were considered to be more costly than effective as means of budgetary management.

2.4 Budget development

Information units' budgeting processes are totally dependent on the type of parent organisation concerned. Generally public library budgets are more detailed given that they operate as complete units and will therefore have to budget for staff, stock purchasing and service costs. On the other hand the industrial or commercial library may not have a direct budget and be charged directly to various accounts within the organisation.

In summary, the development of the information unit budget will be dependent on the methods used in the organisation concerned. Many budgets may be a combination of the budget types outlined above, incorporating cost centres or programmes and line-item budget items (actual types of expenditure).

The following examples illustrate this.

Cost centres might include:

Public Library	Academic Library	Commercial Library (Oil)
Reference library	Technical services group	Exploration
Local studies collection	Circulation services	Development
Central library	Reference desk	Production
Branch libraries	Reader services (main library)	Marketing
Mobile library service	Reader services (branch libraries)	Shipping
		Legal
		Administration Information technology

Budget headings might include:

- payroll costs
- books and monographs
- periodicals, newspapers and serials
- interlibrary loans
- communication costs
- training
- conferences
- office supplies
- accommodation costs such as rents and rates, depreciated cost of owned buildings, cleaning, heating and lighting, contingency planning costs.

Irrespective of the mechanisms used for the budget preparation, the information manager will still have to attach real money figures to the budget. Where cost analysis, discussed in Chapter 3, has been undertaken, figures for staff and overheads will be easily calculated.

It is in the area of the "acquisitions" budget that most problems will arise. Problems here have been complicated in the mid to late 1990s by the move from purchase to access of information, as discussed in Chapter 5. There are problems attached to estimating every element of a normal budget as shown in the following examples.

Books/monographs/maps etc.

• Numbers and subject areas needed.

• Inflation increases, currency increases.

• Average costs vary by subject area: can you obtain published indices for these areas from professional organisations, such as the Cilip, Publishers' Association etc.?

Journals (periodicals)/bibliographic services

• Impact of inflation and currency rates. (A change in the exchange rate for a major purchasing currency can have positive or negative effects on the budget.)

• Periodicals can be a special problem, being longer-term commitments than books. Also note the problems involved in possibly needing to estimate journal prices up to 18 months ahead of commitment – you may be budgeting in mid 2001 for 2003 journals paid for at the end of 2002.

Online and similar services

- Dependent on demand from user community.
- In industrial and commercial organisations how do you manage demand when budgets are fixed?
- How do you cope with the demand for new services or databases introduced by the online industry?
- How do you estimate the costs of printing and downloading?
- What is the impact on hardware budgets for public access equipment of increased usage?
- Should you charge out?
- How should you manage the demand for end-user access?

Much time can be spent on the analysis of the impossible and many acquisitions budgets will inevitably be based to a greater or lesser extent on the information manager's feelings based on past experience and awareness of current patterns – in other words, a guesstimate! Information managers' managers do not always understand the fundamental difficulties involved in this part of the budget cycle.

2.5 Budget presentation

The final outcome of any budgeting process will be a request for funds to the librarian's management team. It is therefore essential that the information unit always keeps a view of the organisation when preparing the budget. During the planning process the information unit will have ensured that it has become aware of:

- the goals of the organisation
- the means by which the organisation accounts itself
- how the information budget compares to the revenues and expenditure of the organisation
- how the information budget relates to those of competitor organisations
- the value that the information unit provides to the organisation.

The written budget submission should provide:

- sufficient background data relating to the information unit
- a brief discussion of the plans for the period concerned
- the budget itself together with appropriate historical information
- the phased breakdown of expenditure.

Formal presentation of the budget is the key to the manager's success and methods will depend on the organisation concerned and may indeed change from financial year to financial year within the same organisation. In the broadest sense the information manager will be 'selling' his service throughout the budget process.

Appendix A provides selective parts of a budget proposal presented to a company as part of its budget cycle.

Phasing is an important part of the budget exercise as the total expenditure budgeted for the information unit will not be spent in 12 equal instalments, relating to each of the calendar months of the year.

There is therefore a need for a cash budget, discussed in a later section.

In most commercial libraries periodicals, for instance, will be purchased (or at least paid for) in one major billing, often in November or December where subscriptions run on a calendar year. Taking the example in Figure 1 it would be essential that the periodicals fund is correctly phased otherwise misleading management information would be reported throughout the year. The cash budget, Figure 6, illustrates phasing at work. The level of phasing will depend on an individual organisation's reporting cycle. It must be noted that not all automated accounting procedures will actually allow for phasing to be built in at the level of detail applicable to the information unit. The decision must then be made whether or not to construct an internal financial model for the unit – as illustrated in Figure 4.

Whichever budget methodology is used it is essential that the overall budget submission is packaged and presented in a style that will mean it is well

XYZ Company Limited   Information Centre   Budget preparation 2002

Description	Jan	Feb	Mar	Apr	May	Jun	Jul	Aug	Sep	Oct	Nov	Dec
	9-5	9-5	9-5	9-5	9-5	9-5	9-5	9-5	9-5	9-5	9-5	9-5
Employee Costs												
Payroll Costs (Permanent Staff)	15750	31500	47250	63000	78750	94500	110250	126000	141750	157500	173250	189000
Payroll Costs (Contract Staff)	8312.5	16625	24937.5	33250	41562.5	49875	58187.5	66500	74812.5	83125	91437.5	99750
Fringe Benefits	7175	14350	21525	28700	35875	43050	50225	57400	64575	71750	78925	86100
Overtime	875	1750	2625	3500	4375	5250	6125	7000	7875	8750	9625	10500
Company NIC	1872.5	3745	5617.5	7490	9362.5	11235	13107.5	14980	16852.5	18725	20597.5	22470
Total Employee Costs	33985	67970	101955	135940	169925	203910	237895	271880	305865	339850	373835	407820
Departmental Overhead Costs												
Books and Monographs	2580	5165	7745	10330	12910	15495	18080	20665	23245	25830	28415	31000
Journals	1450	2900	4350	5800	7250	8700	10150	11600	13050	14500	84500	86000
Newspapers & Press Cuttings	2080	4165	6245	8330	10410	12495	14575	16660	18740	20825	22905	25000
Online Services (call-off)	2915	5830	8745	11660	14375	17490	20405	23320	26235	29150	32065	35000
Online Services (current awareness)	415	830	1245	1660	2075	2490	2905	3320	3735	4150	4565	5000
Scouting Services	6875	6875	6875	13750	13750	13750	20625	20625	20625	27500	27500	27500
Maps	200	400	600	800	1000	1200	1400	1600	1800	2100	2300	2500
Bibliographic & Indexing Tools	0	0	0	0	0	0	0	0	0	0	2100	2100
Total Publications	16515	26165	35805	52330	61770	71620	88140	97700	107430	124055	204350	214100
Data Storage Costs	0	51667	51667	103334	103334	155001	155001	206667	206667	258334	258334	310000
Computing Services Recharged	5000	10000	15000	20000	25000	30000	35000	40000	45000	50000	55000	60000
Total Departmental Overheads	21515	87832	102472	175664	190104	256621	278141	344457	359097	432389	517684	584100
Business Expenses												
Professional Fees/consultants	700	850	1000	1150	1300	1450	1600	1750	1900	2050	2450	2500
Travel (Staff)	225	450	675	900	1125	1350	1575	1800	2025	2250	2500	2700
Accommodation & Subsidence (Staff)	125	250	375	500	675	800	925	1050	1175	1300	1425	1500
Entertainment (Non-staff)	80	165	250	335	415	500	580	665	745	850	935	1000
Staff Conferences	0	0	0	0	0	0	3000	3000	3000	3000	3000	3000
Total Business Expenses	1130	1715	2300	2885	3515	4100	7680	8265	8845	9450	10310	10700
Allocated Overheads - Office Space	5743.75	11475.25	17219.25	22963	28708.75	34460.5	40194.25	45938	51681.75	57425.5	63169.25	68925
Allocated Overheads - Office Services	5068.5	10137	15205.5	20274	25342.5	30411	35479.5	40548	45616.5	50685	55753.5	60825
Allocated Overheads - Personnel	1006.167	2012.34	3018.51	4024.68	5030.85	6037.02	7043.19	8049.36	9055.53	10061.7	11067.87	12074
Allocated Overheads - Finance	141.92	283.54	425.46	567.38	709.3	851.22	993.14	1135.06	1276.98	1418.9	1560.82	1703
Total Allocated Overheads	12890.34	25768.38	38658.72	51549.06	64439.4	77329.74	90220.08	103110.42	116000.76	128891.1	141791.44	154684
Total Cost Centre	69520.34	183285.38	245386.72	366038.06	659283.4	541960.74	613636.08	727732.42	789807.76	910580.1	1043820.44	1157304

Figure 4:   Internal Financial Model for LIS Unit

received by management. The information manager should:

- ensure brevity and simplicity
- provide explanations for all changes in the budget, both increases and reductions
- relate the budget and goals of the information unit to those of the parent organisation
- be honest in all dealings with management
- be aware and have an understanding of the needs of other parts of the organisation for resource allocations
- ensure that the organisation is aware of the service available from the information unit.

2.6 Budget timetables

The financial management process is a continuing series of 'curves' which can be entered at any point. Figure 5 illustrates the inter-relationship of the various cycles involved from budgeting to expenditure, to reporting and analysis, which is the order of topics covered in this volume. It will be obvious from Figure 5, that the library and information service professional will be generally working on at least two budget cycles at most times of the year.

Budget timetables will be set for the organisation as a whole as shown in Table 1.

Table 1: Sample budget timetable

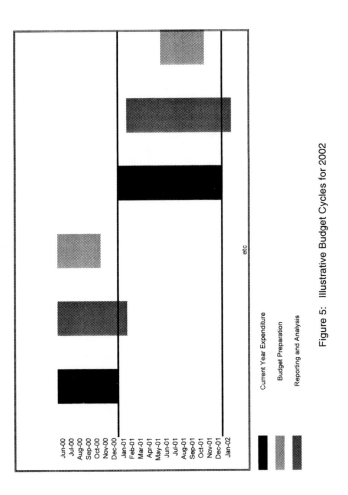

Figure 5: Illustrative Budget Cycles for 2002

The sample timetable includes the bland statement that departmental budgets would be agreed by the end of September. The process of management approval is not so easy and, in order to guarantee that

Table 1: Sample budget timetable

Date	Activity	Responsibility
May 31st	Manpower figures discussed	Departmental
June 30th	Manpower figures agreed	Management
July 31st	Allocated service overheads agreed	Accountants
Aug. 31st	Departmental overheads prepared	Departmental
Sep. 30th	Overall departmental budgets prepared	Departmental
Oct.	Consideration of all departmental bids	Management
Oct. 31st	Final corporate budget approved	Management
Nov. 30th	Approved departmental budgets issued	Accountants
Dec. 5th	Compare allocation with bid implement changes	Departmental

Departmental = Information unit manager
Accountants = Central financial authorities
Management = The information unit's management, i.e. the organisational process

the budget stands the best possible chance of survival in the form that the information manager wishes, the manager must ensure that:

- he or she is sure of their ground and can provide answers to the questions that will be asked during the review
- the basis for inflation calculations can be explained
- where average book and/or serial prices are used, their basis of calculation is understood or can at least be produced

- he or she can explain the consequences of any reductions proposed in the budget submission.

Even where the departmental budget has been agreed there is no guarantee that the organisation's management will be able to approve any particular single departmental budget. It is quite possible that when all departmental budgets are consolidated into the company budget the overall figures may not be acceptable. The organisation may not be able to afford all the bids for any number of reasons – production, markets and prices or financial. At this point the *cash budget* becomes the most significant budget in the organisation.

2.7 Cash budgeting

In the commercial environment services are generally not paid for on a day-to-day cash basis. Organisations give and receive credit, supplies are ordered which are paid for at some time after receipt, and goods are supplied for which payment will be received at a later date.

At the **organisational accounting level** the final product of the budget process will be the *budgeted balance sheet.* The inter-related components of this balance sheet are shown in Table 2.

Table 2: Budgeted balance sheet

Overhead	Labour	Materials	Expenses

Research & Development Budget	Administration Budget	Production Budget	Marketing & Sales Costs Budget

Cash Budget	Budgeted Profit & Loss Account	Capital Expenditure Budget	Stock Budget

Budgeted Balance Sheet

The cash budget is probably the most important budget within the organisation as it is the budget that expresses all the underlying departmental budgets into cash flow terms. Cash budgets show when receipt of income is expected and when expenses will be incurred. Once all the departmental and other budgets are consolidated into the cash budget the organisation may find that the financing of a particular level of a specified activity may not be possible. This is because the organisation has overall financial constraints and the fundamental need to make profits or at least to stay within the financial constraints of the organisation's paymasters.

The cash budget is important as it not only reflects the cash impact of budget plans but also provides an indication of the surpluses and deficits allowing for cash management.

Figure 6 presents the Line-Item Budget from Figure 1 in cash budget format. As can be seen, the cash budget has precisely the same headings as the budget but also records when expenditure is expected to occur.

XYZ Company Limited   Information Centre   Budget preparation 2002

Description	Total	Jan	Feb	Mar	Apr	May	Jun	Jul	Aug	Sep	Oct	Nov	Dec
	9+5	9+5	9+5	9+5	9+5	9+5	9+5	9+5	9+5	9+5	9+5	9+5	9+5
Employee Costs													
Payroll Costs (Permanent Staff)	189000	15750	15750	15750	15750	15750	15750	15750	15750	15750	15750	15750	15750
Payroll Costs (Contract Staff)	99750	8312.5	8312.5	8312.5	8312.5	8312.5	8312.5	8312.5	8312.5	8312.5	8312.5	8312.5	8312.5
Fringe Benefits	86100	7175	7175	7175	7175	7175	7175	7175	7175	7175	7175	7175	7175
Overtime	10500	875	875	875	875	875	875	875	875	875	875	875	875
Company NIC	22470	1872.5	1872.5	1872.5	1872.5	1872.5	1872.5	1872.5	1872.5	1872.5	1872.5	1872.5	1872.5
Total Employee Costs	407820	33985	33985	33985	33985	33985	33985	33985	33985	33985	33985	33985	33985
Departmental Overhead Costs													
Books and Monographs	31000	2585	2585	2585	2585	2585	2585	2585	2585	2585	2580	2585	2585
Journals	18000	1450	1450	1450	1450	1450	1450	1450	1450	1450	1450	70000	1450
Newspapers & Press Cuttings	25000	2080	2080	2080	2080	2080	2080	2080	2080	2080	2080	2080	2080
Online Services (call-off)	35000	2915	2915	2915	2915	2915	2915	2915	2915	2915	2915	2915	2915
Online Services (current awareness)	5000	415	415	415	415	415	415	415	415	415	415	415	435
Scouting Services	27500	6875	0	0	6875	0	0	6875	0	0	6875	0	0
Maps	2600	200	0	200	200	0	200	200	200	200	200	300	200
Bibliographic & Indexing Tools	2100	0	0	0	0	0	0	0	0	0	0	2100	0
Total Publications	214100	16515	9650	9650	9640	9640	9650	16620	9650	9650	9640	80296	9750
Data Storage Costs	310000	0	51667	51667	0	51667	51667	51687	51696	51996	0	0	51666
Computing Services Recharged	60000	5000	5000	5000	5000	5000	5000	5000	5000	5000	5000	5000	5000
Total Departmental Overheads	584100	21515	66317	66317	14640	14640	66317	21520	66316	14640	14640	85295	66416
Business Expenses													
Professional Fees-consultants	2500	700	150	150	150	150	150	150	150	150	150	300	150
Travel (Staff)	2700	225	225	225	225	225	225	225	225	225	225	225	225
Accommodation & Subsistence (Staff)	1500	125	125	125	125	125	125	125	125	125	125	125	125
Entertainment (Non-staff)	1000	80	85	85	85	80	80	85	90	85	85	85	85
Staff Conferences	3000	0	0	0	0	0	0	0	3000	0	0	0	0
Total Business Expenses	10700	1130	585	585	585	580	580	585	3580	585	580	735	585
Allocated Overheads - Office Space	68925	5743.75	5743.75	5743.75	5743.75	5743.75	5743.75	5743.75	5743.75	5743.75	5743.75	5743.75	5743.75
Allocated Overheads - Office Services	71982	5998.5	5998.5	5998.5	5998.5	5998.5	5998.5	5998.5	5998.5	5998.5	5998.5	5998.5	5998.5
Allocated Overheads - Personnel	12074	1006.166967	1006.166967	1006.166967	1006.166967	1006.166967	1006.166967	1006.166967	1006.166967	1006.166967	1006.166967	1006.166967	1006.166967
Allocated Overheads - Finance	1703	141.92	141.92	141.92	141.92	141.92	141.92	141.92	141.92	141.92	141.92	141.92	141.88
Total Allocated Overheads	154694	12890.33667	12890.33667	12890.33667	12890.33667	12890.33667	12890.33667	12890.33667	12890.33667	12890.33667	12890.33667	12890.33667	12890.29667
Total Cost Centre	1157304	125020.3367	113777.3367	113777.3367	120652.3367	62095.3367	113777.3367	71975.3367	113776.3387	62095.3367	120752.3367	132905.9367	113876.2967

Figure 6:   Line-Item Budget presented as Cash Budget

2.8 Budget expenditure

Having established the budget, the information manager will now wish to spend the resources. Spending other people's money naturally has rules attached to it. These will depend on the organisation concerned and will be documented in the corporate procedures of the organisation.

The procedures will ensure that:

- expenditure is justified as valid and fulfilling the aims and goals of the organisation
- only those goods which are actually received are paid for – in information units this can cause administrative headaches given the numerous instances where prepayment is required, ranging from other organisations' natural unwillingness to invoice amounts of £10 to the need to spend periodical subscriptions before the first issue is received
- the accounts department charges the correct cost centre and detail code
- year-end financial administration is carried out in the correct fashion.

3. Costing

It must be emphasised that the techniques of costing are simply concerned with matters of fact – all activities can be costed. Using the costs derived is a matter for policy-makers and guidance on this area is provided in Webb (17) and other works on charging for library and information units.

The finished output of a costing exercise will be clear, detailed (or summary dependent on management reporting level) and timely information. Any costing system that cannot fulfil these requirements at reasonable cost is of no value to the information manager.

Historically many organisations have simply funded their information units on the basis of historical allotment. Roberts (3a, b) outlined a number of reasons why cost analysis had not been implemented by 1985 in many library and information units:

- lack of financial expertise in the information unit
- public accountability had not been 'particularly onerous' for libraries
- historical lack of financial and managerial accountability in libraries
- library management style is more often subjective than objective.

However, in these days of stringency, information managers are likely to be faced with, at the very least, a need to be seen to control and justify costs or, at worst, the need to recover costs. Consequently cost analysis has become a vital part of the financial management armoury that information managers use when defending and justifying the service and costs of their units. Knowledge of the true costs of library functions ensures that the information manager is able to consider alternative means of supplying the service required. Such knowledge also allows the funding management to be convinced that the unit is providing value for money. Even when a full costing exercise has been undertaken the fact that the 'true' cost of a service is known does not mean that the service itself is justified.

Where the information manager initiates the costing exercise he or she is able to take the initiative when competing for funds and the costing exercise forms an essential part of the planning process.

As has been seen in Chapter 2, the actual costs of materials supplied as part of the information service form only a minor part of the overall information budget. This is shown in Figure 1, which is summarised in Table 3 below.

Table 3 – Broad analysis of line budgets

Employee costs	35.2%
Publications	17.3%
Other departmental overheads	33.4%
Business expenses	1.1%
Allocated overheads	12.9%

Were these figures from the example budget (Figure 1) recalculated to exclude the data storage charges the result would be a payroll figure costing around 49 per cent of the total cost of the department. This confirms that in most information units employee costs are the largest single cost – information work is and will continue to be staff intensive.

3.1 Performance measures

With the benefit of practical experience I can agree with McLean (18) who notes that one of the reasons for the problems that information managers have in applying cost evaluation techniques to their units is the fact that 'performance measures are intrinsically related to the perceptions of users'.

In an effort to provide measures of use to library and information units during cost and performance evaluation exercises the Office of Arts and Libraries (OAL) has published a manual (19) which identifies 21 performance measures grouped into four types:

1. Input cost:
    - amount of resources applied to service
    - amount of funding applied to services
    - relevant attributes of resources applied to services.
2. Output measures:
    - quantities of output
    - quality of output
    - timelessness of output
    - availability of service

- accessibility of service.
3.	Service effectiveness measures:
	- amount of use
	- user perception of outputs
	- user expressed satisfaction
	- user indicated importance
	- purpose of use
	- consequence of use.
4.	Service domain measures:
	- total population size
	- total population attributes
	- user population size
	- user population attributes
	- size of geographic area
	- geographic area attributes
	- information needs.

3.2 Cost accounting

Cost accounting is the process of allocating resources to activities to show the cost of each individual activity. The techniques and results of a cost accounting exercise will assist the information manager in a variety of activities. They will:

- specify the cost structure, illustrating how the budget is made up (employee costs, departmental overheads, business expenses) and how it is spent or allocated by the functions undertaken by the information unit (library services, information services and data management services)

- help with supervising the efficiency of operations
- provide information allowing the calculation of service prices
- provide pricing aids allowing for decisions in relation to in-house provision or contracting out
- allow comparison of cost between different information systems
- allow new or changed services to be costed
- aid review of financial performance
- help in the preparation of budgets
- assist in re-planning and re-budgeting exercises.

3.3 Cost analysis

The cost analysis process involves a series of steps.

- identification of cost centres
- listing of employee activities
- selection of unit measures of output and period during analysis will take place
- designing of paperwork and computer systems for staff to use for recording purposes
- ensuring that staff record ALL activities
- generation of monthly summaries of employee activities
- production of annual estimates for each employee
- calculation of cost of employee activities
- consolidation of data to each cost centre
- allocation of non-personnel overhead costs

- allocation of indirect expenses
- determination of unit cost of each unit measure
- reconciliation of costs determined during survey with operating costs for unit.

Identification of cost centres

Cost centres will depend on the level of cost analysis being undertaken and would range from those covering all aspects of the information unit to those covering a single department or function such as a records centre or the acquisitions section.

Listing of employee activities

Decide the activities to be analysed. Various lists of library tasks have been published, e.g. by Clements (20), Beecher et al (21a, b) and Mitchell et al (22), but it is essential that any listing is applicable to the department being analysed – do not simply use a published list without thought. For example, the acquisitions function would include areas such as:

- ordering, receiving and payment functions
- cataloguing including checking past editions, headings etc.
- preparation of the volumes for circulation or addition to the collections
- maintenance of the catalogue databases.

All these areas would be broken down into a series of specific tasks.

Selection of unit measures of output

These will depend on the nature of the unit being costed; for instance the number of volumes catalogued; the number of online searches undertaken, the number of periodical parts received. One such list is provided by OAL (19), section 5.6.

Designing of paperwork and computer systems for staff to use for recording purposes

It is essential that any systems that are used for recording purposes are both easy to use and easy to analyse. Accurate data is essential for costing exercises and can only be obtained by accurate data collection.

Ensuring that staff record ALL activities

There are many ways of recording staff activities. In commercial organisations where staff will often be timewriting for general purposes it would be possible to extend the system to specific library tasks for the duration of the survey period. Timewriting is, however, just one method of ensuring that staff time can be allocated to the cost centre (or tasks) that are being analysed. Other methods which will produce a similar analysis include: continuous time observation study (the traditional time and motion technique), work sampling, diary keeping and RAM (Random Alarm Sampling), Beecher et al (21a, b). This last technique originates and appears to be used solely in the United States.

Generation of monthly summaries of employee activities

When analysing staff activities it is essential that any unusual, non-periodic activities are recorded, and accounted for.

Production of annual estimates for each employee

Employee costs must include their full costs, i.e. payroll, fringe benefits, overtime and company National Insurance. Because no employee works 52 times their weekly hours, many organisations, particularly in industry, will have a fixed yearly hours total that is used for the calculation of hourly rates.

Calculation of cost of employee activities

Hourly staff costs are determined using the equation:

$$\text{Hourly rate} = \frac{\Sigma \, (\text{Salary} + \text{Fringe benefits} + \text{Company NIC})}{\text{Effective hours total}}$$

The effective hours total may be calculated either on the basis of an organisationally specified rate which would allow for an agreed number of hours or be calculated by assuming fixed rates for training, illness, public holidays, annual leave and weekends.

Consolidation of data to each cost centre

Non-personnel costs represent the cost of materials that can be specifically assigned to the task being costed. For instance, where an information service is being costed in its entirety, the costs of online information services would be included; in the case of cataloguing, the costs of checking the local bibliographic database would be charged to it.

Allocation of indirect expenses

The range of items included in 'allocated indirect expenses' will depend on the organisation's specific methods for allocating such expenses. In some organisations all office overheads will be allocated out by space and or staff numbers. This is illustrated in the allocated overheads' line that appears in Figure 1, and in other figures given as examples in this publication. Although not explicitly noted in the budget, the office services budget would include expenses ranging from telephone/telex costs to office supplies and the office space allocation would include power and heating charges. It should be noted that where office overheads are calculated on floor space bases information units will invariably have high indirect costs.

The full range of indirect costs include:

- hired equipment
- maintenance and repairs
- recruitment costs, relocation services
- medical facilities
- sports facilities
- telephone, telex and other communication costs
- accommodation costs (including cleaning, rates)
- utilities (gas, electricity, water)
- bank charges

- sponsorship and donations
- insurance
- security.

Determination of unit cost of each unit measure

Unit cost is simply calculated as:

$$\frac{\text{Total cost of producing X units}}{X}$$

During any costing exercise it is essential that the information manager is aware of the various types of costs that will be encountered and which will affect the cost analysis process.

- Direct costs are those directly incurred by the information units, for instance, the cost of journals purchased for stock.

- Indirect costs are those that cannot be directly controlled by the information manager and which will generally apply to a number of cost centres within the organisation, for instance, the cost of building services.

- Fixed costs are those that do not change with volume. In an information unit the cost of the space occupied by the unit is not dependent on how much the department is used (at least in general terms; the information unit will occupy the same space unless major changes are forced upon it).

- Variable costs are those that are dependent on the level of activities undertaken. The number of online searches may double to cater for user demands, and their costs will rise in proportion.

So it can be seen that the cost analysis produces significant quantities of basic data that can be used by information managers for a variety of purposes. In the twenty-first century, I would expect that their primary use would be in the area of calculation of rates for use during the charging out process. This may be based on a number of methods:

- total costs, including direct and indirect
- direct costs only – the simplest means of cost recovery
- flat fee, as may be used in public libraries, to cover some or all of the costs
- sliding scale fees where some users may be subsidised by others.

4. Financial reporting and accounting

Just as budgeting is the first stage in the financial process, financial reporting is the final stage and is totally bound up with the expenditure process. At its simplest the financial reporting exercise can be seen as the means by which the financially efficient manager *will be able to answer, without the need to spend hours in calculation,* the question: 'What level of resource *remains* available to this information unit?'

The answer is derived from one of the three forms of the 'basic financial equation':

Available expenditure (balance) = BUDGET - Actual to date – Committed to date

but the figures need to be available from the financial systems.

4.1 Basic bookkeeping

To ensure that the information manager can obtain the financial information required to solve the basic financial equation, the information systems used for bookkeeping within the information function must allow for commitment expenditure. This functionality is developed in more detail in the section on spreadsheets (Chapter 6). Here it is enough to stress that the information unit must have a means of accounting that ensures that account is taken of all orders issued but not received at any particular time. Particular problems may be encountered with serial/

journal publications and with standing orders for continuing series and also with irregularly published monographic series where the publication frequency and price cannot be determined in advance. Automated acquisition systems, which are found in many libraries, can take some of the routine work out of the financial management process.

4.2 Accounting

Accounting is the term that describes the processes involved in the measurement and recording of financial information and its subsequent communication and interpretation as background to decision-making within the organisation at all levels.

Three types of accounting are recognised by the accounting profession:

- financial accounting
- cost accounting
- management accounting.

Financial accounts are the most common type of accounts and can be seen in the financial reporting deposited at Companies House by all companies from partnerships to plcs. The accounts record the transactions of the organisation with third parties, such as suppliers, customers and of course their staff.

Cost accounts record the internal activities of the organisation and although the methodology originated in the manufacturing industry they are now being produced in organisations of all types. In simple terms cost accounting is the process of establishing the cost in money terms of the activity or process being reviewed.

Management accounting is a process combining financial and cost accounting that provides the complete picture of the financial state of the organisation and should allow the organisation's management to manage its finances prudently.

4.3 Accounting cycles

In order to present financial information for management use the accounting function works in a cyclic fashion undertaking the steps shown in Table 4.

Table 4: Accounting cycles

Function/Step	Procedure involved	Frequency
Transaction analysis	Code payments/receipts to appropriate cost centres	Daily
Transfer transactions to journals	The entry of transactions into the accounting system	Daily
Post journals to ledgers	Transfer of data from journals to ledgers	Monthly
Post posting adjustments	Adjustments (corrections) to transactions. At year end would also include the process of accruing expenses – where payments made in the following cash year are charged to the preceding year for goods that have been received	Annually [Monthly]
Preparation of trial balance	Totals of all debits and credits to ensure that the figures balance acts as a check on transaction processing	Monthly
Preparation of financial statements	Production at regular, generally monthly, intervals of financial reports	Monthly Annually
Prepare closing entries	Year end process, which closes accounts at the end of the fiscal year, prior to production of final closing balance	Annually
Preparation of final (closing) trial balance	Year end operation to produce final fund accounting reports	Annually

4.4 Financial reports

Financial reports fall into three categories definable by the way in which information is provided:

- those which provide information and reporting
- those which examine

- those which analyse.

There is an endless range of permutations for financial reports, since it is possible to analyse a set of figures in any number of ways. Within the information unit there will be a wide variety of financial reports available to assist the information manager with his or her work on the 'basic equation'.

All financial reports will, however, show a variety of features in so far as they will be:

- **timely**: reports are needed shortly after the period to which they refer, not months later when it would be too late to take action to solve any financial problems highlighted

- **accurate**: all reports should be auditable; for instance, the first level cost centre report would be supported by detailed listings of transactions allocated to the cost centre concerned

- **relevant**: reports should only contain information of use to those receiving the report

- **cost effective**: reports should not be generated where their cost exceeds the financial benefits of having the reported information.

The most widely used financial reports are the following.

- Summary statements of financial conditions are the basic report providing details of the financial situation of the information unit and will be supported by one or more of the other types of report.

- Reports analysing changes in financial conditions, which allow reporting of significant variances between the sums budgeted and the levels of expenditure.

- 'Actuals' position to date are detailed report's covering many or all of the transactions charged to a specific cost centre.

- Measures of efficiency levels reports will be produced in information units that use PPBS or other systems which measure outputs. Accountants will be able to produce costs relating to particular programmes and then the information manager can compare actual and planned performance across the information unit or individual activities.

- Capital expenditure reports are used in most organisations to report expenditure on items to be depreciated and included in the 'capital expenditure' budget, in a separate reporting cycle.

- 'Special' funding reports are used in institutions which have funds allocated for specific and special purposes and need to report expenditure and income on these separately.

4.5 Budget variances

The fundamental use of financial reporting is to ensure that expenditure can be monitored against budget thus allowing managers to take appropriate action where expenditure is over or under the agreed budget.

Actual expenditure may be compared against either the formal departmental budgets or against the departmental cash budget, see Figure 7.

XYZ Company Limited   Information Centre   Budget Reporting Year to
February 2002

	A	B	C	D	E	F
1	Description	Budget to date	Expenditure to Date	Variance		[+/10%]
2						
3						
4	Employee Costs					
5	Payroll Costs (Permanent Staff)	31500	31450	-50		
6	Payroll Costs (Contract Staff)	16625	16625	0		
7	Fringe Benefits	14350	14350	0		
8	Overtime	1750	500	-1250		****
9	Company NIC	3745	3740	-5		
10						
11	Total Employee Costs	67970	66665	-1305		
12						
13	Departmental Overhead Costs					
14						
15	Books and Monographs	5165	5500	335		
16	Journals	2900	2790	-110		
17	Newspapers & Press Cuttings	4165	4165	0		
18	Online Services (call-off)	5830	6500	670		****
19	Online Services (current awareness)	830	830	0		
20	Scouting Services	6875	7000	125		
21	Maps	400	150	-250		
22	Bibliographic & Indexing Tools	0	0	0		
23						
24	Total Publications	26165	26935	770		
25						
26	Data Storage Costs	51667	51667	0		
27	Computing Services Recharged	10000	8500	-1500		
28						
29	Total Departmental Overheads	87832	87102	-730		
30						
31	Business Expenses					
32						
33	Professional Fees/consultants	850	0	-850		****
34	Travel (Staff)	450	580	130		****
35	Accommodation & Subsidence (Staff)	250	125	-125		****
36	Entertainment (Non-staff)	165	0	-165		****
37	Staff Conferences	0	0	0		
38						
39	Total Business Expenses	1715	705	-1010		
40						
41	Allocated Overheads - Office Space	11487.5	11487.5	0		
42	Allocated Overheads - Office Services	11997	11997	0		
43	Allocated Overheads - Personnel	2012.33	2012.33	0		
44	Allocated Overheads - Finance	283.84	283.84	0		
45						
46	Total Allocated Overheads	25780	25780	0		
47						
48	Total Cost Centre	183297	180252	-3045		
49						

Figure 7:   Illustrative Financial Report

This financial report presents financial information in six columns. Column A lists the headings under which the budget is compiled and managed. Column B presents the budget to the date of the report, in this case the first two months. Column C presents the charged expenditure to date whilst the variance between budget and expenditure is presented in column D. The XYZ Company Limited uses a plus or minus 10 per cent variance basis, and column F highlights those expenditure categories for which the variance is outwith the standard, and for which the information manager would need to account.

Irrespective of whether a budget is overspent or underspent the variances are a matter for concern. Many commercial organisations permit managers to have a variance of plus or minus 10 per cent on their budget; outwith this variance, comprehensive justification and explanation will be required.

Negative variances, where expenditure exceeds budget, may be caused by:

- changing situations, for example, a new project may start which requires additional information resources
- inappropriate plans
- unavoidable expenditures, for example, computers may have to be replaced; office accommodation charges may be changed
- charges may be paid in the wrong financial period – documents may be invoiced too late to be paid in the correct financial year.

Reversing these factors would result in a positive variance (underspending the budget). Another reason for underspending might be the unavailability of publications.

Naturally negative variances are of more immediate concern to the information manager since prompt action may be needed to prevent the budget continuing to be overspent.

The original budgets will have been prepared, in an accounting sense, on either a fixed or flexible basis. Where a fixed budget policy is adopted actual results will be compared against the budget. Flexible budgeting operates on the principle that budgets may be adjusted on the basis of changes that have taken place since the budget was compiled. The actual results are then compared against this 'flexed' budget, which consequently allows for better consideration of any variances against the budget. In manufacturing terms if production increases then so will sales. However, increased production will result in higher production costs, resulting in a negative variance against budget, whilst the increased sales will show a positive variance. Flexible budgeting will ensure that actual performance is analysed against the most accurate figures.

The organisation may permit transfers between budget headings where over and under spending can be netted out; otherwise in the most severe circumstances it may be necessary to cease all optional expenditure – for instance continue to pay permanent staff whilst cancelling book orders and terminating contract staff.

4.6 Corporate reporting

Whilst it goes without saying that the financial information contained in any sequence of financial reports will be the same, the method of presentation will depend on the audience concerned. In a corporate reporting environment a sequence of reports would be generated with each succeeding level containing less detailed information:

- cost centre transactional listing
- cost centre fund analysis
- cost centre total (information manager's report)
- functional group total
- divisional or subsidiary total
- corporate total
- published profit and loss account.

Cost centre transactional listing

This is the detailed listing of all payments and receipts relating to the cost centre. An example may be seen in the upper part of Figure 8.

Cost centre fund analysis

This is consolidated listing of payments and receipts analysed by the funds defined in a cost centre's budget. An example may be seen in the lower part of Figure 8.

XYZ Company Limited   Transaction Listing   Library

	Date	Payment	Invoice	Supplier	Amount
76X89D	4-Nov-94	987163	S795971	Crier Books	£145.96
76X89D	4-Nov-94	987166	S793457	Crier Books	£150.00
76X89D	4-Nov-94	987167	725726B	Butterfield	£65.00
76X89D	5-Nov-94	987212	55369054	HMSO	£15.00
76X89D	8-Nov-94	987165	B793793	Crier Books	£25.95
76X89D	8-Nov-94	987256	B793790	Crier Books	£27.99
76X89D	9-Nov-94	987164	B793794	Crier Books	£24.95
76X89D	9-Nov-94	987340	A94269	McKay & Son	£200.00
76X89D	9-Nov-94	987341	A94271	McKay & Son	£20.00
76X89D	12-Nov-94	987045	A94254	McKay & Son	£115.00
76X89D	12-Nov-94	987364	704169B	Butterworths	£180.00
76X89D	12-Nov-94	987483	34645406	HMSO	£20.00
76X89D	12-Nov-94	987514	34645762	HMSO	£16.10
76X89D	13-Nov-94	987544	B4504097	Crier Books	£45.00
76X89D	14-Nov-94	987560	X4504097	Crier Books	£22.00
76X89D	16-Nov-94	987042	B790655	Crier Books	£140.00
76X89D	19-Nov-94	987011	S791632	Crier Books	£7.50
76X89D	22-Nov-94	987005	1-4456459	Jaeger & Waldmar	£1,171.86
76X89D	22-Nov-94	987043	S7916245	Crier Books	£160.00
76X89D	24-Nov-94	987821	S983	IPPR	£9.95
76X89D	25-Nov-94	987841	A94363	McKay & Son	£100.00
76X92E	2-Nov-94	987088	1051903	McGee Publishing	£95.00
76X92E	3-Nov-94	987095	14574515	Crier Subscriptions	£297.00
76X92E	3-Nov-94	987096	14574515	Crier Subscriptions	£39.00
76X92E	8-Nov-94	987254	B793788	Crier Books	£27.50
76X92E	9-Nov-94	987245	B793802	Crier Books	£55.00
76X92E	9-Nov-94	987346	B793796	Crier Books	£0.00
76X92E	22-Nov-94	987569	A94345	McKay & Son	£117.50
76X92E	22-Nov-94	987800	A94346	McKay & Son	£20.00
76X92E	24-Nov-94	987810	94/204	African Gas Market Report	£45.00
76X92E	24-Nov-94	987820	A94356	McKay & Son	£50.00
76X92E	25-Nov-94	987840	A94362	McKay & Son	£40.00
76X92E	28-Nov-94	987860	34645987	HMSO	£19.95
76X92Q	1-Nov-94	987083	A94254	McKay & Son	£25.00
76X92Q	3-Nov-94	987097	14574516	Crier Subscriptions	£146.25
76X92Q	8-Nov-94	987255	A94267	McKay & Son	£32.00
76X92Q	9-Nov-94	987345	34645776	HMSO	£50.00
76X92Q	9-Nov-94	987347	B793810	Crier Books	£86.00
76X92Q	12-Nov-94	987046	55369169	HMSO	£255.50
76X92Q	17-Nov-94	987565	A94324	McKay & Son	£75.00
76X92Q	26-Nov-94	987850	234	IT Management Reports	£682.00
	November		76X89D		£2,662.26
	November		76X92E		£805.95
	November		76X92Q		£1,351.75

Figure 8:   LIS Unit Transaction Report (Accounting Generated)

Cost centre total (information manager's report)

The information manager's report, Figure 7, will of course be detailed and will provide a breakdown of expenditure against budget headings. The manager's report will include a full explanation of the variances between budgeted and actual expenditure. Additionally the report will give projections of expenditure to the end of the fiscal year; reports may also give comparisons with the previous year.

Functional group total, Divisional or subsidiary total, Corporate total

Depending on the structure of the organisation, various levels of consolidated reporting are possible. Hypothetically the reporting structure could be:

- *Functional group total:* this report might be produced for information management, which includes the information unit, and is one of six business units within the company.

- *Divisional/subsidiary total*: this report might be produced for a UK subsidiary company.

- *Corporate total*: this might be prepared for a US parent company.

Published profit and loss account

This forms part of the published accounts of the organisation deposited at Companies House or its equivalent.

5. Information access versus purchase

All libraries and information units have been in a period of transition since the mid-1990s as the need to consider the relationship between access and purchase has become increasingly significant.

Many sources that were once only available in a hard copy, traditionally published, format are now available in printed, CD-ROM and online electronic format.

Information units need to make informed choices between varying formats, different payment mechanisms, and indeed different access methods. All these choices will have an impact on the library's budget and financial management processes. Many librarians believe that given the escalating price and rapid growth in the numbers of both electronic publications and their hard copy equivalents, information units will be forced to choose between electronic and print products in the early years of the new millennium. Indeed the library at Drexel was planning in 1998 to migrate fully to electronic publications wherever possible. Montgomery and Sparks (23) provide an excellent review of the process at Drexel, with their Table 1 summarising the impact of the changes to staffing and other costs of the exercise. The final paragraph is also worth noting:

> In summary while the cost of providing … has increased our expenditures overall, unit costs have significantly decreased since we now provide a collection that is almost four times larger and far more heavily used. We know we are obtaining a better return on investment … but at this early stage the magnitude cannot be calculated precisely.

As electronic resources develop, alternatives to outright purchasing have begun invading budgets as the providers of such information have found it increasingly advantageous to use either contracts or leases to cover the library use of their products.

One of the major but little mentioned reasons for this is that most of the contents of such compilations or databases are not subject to copyright but are in the public domain. Under any purchase agreement, the library could make unlimited use of the database. Of course, this statement overlooks the intellectual and financial investment in creating the database, but the provider is thus forced to look for other ways to recoup development costs. In situations involving contracts or leases nothing changes hands as it does with a purchase, but the lessee or contractee has to abide by whatever conditions are established.

With the growth of electronic publications and services, this kind of relationship has expanded rapidly and librarians now find themselves as much involved in negotiating leases and contracts as with simple purchase. In fact, the involvement may even be greater when it becomes necessary to consult lawyers and other specialists about the terms of a contract or lease.

With any electronic resource, libraries may find that they are required to pay a basic fee regardless of use or that each use incurs some kind of overhead. In addition there are also likely to be provisions attached to any contract negotiated, as to how the information is to be used or shared. The information specialist is likely to find her or himself as the middleperson in a wide range of transactions between the information users and the information provider, this being especially true in 'special' libraries and information units.

Any and all of these situations affect the library's budget and its distribution. As Friend (24) notes:

> the availability of networked information resources provides the opportunity for a new financial model to develop ... The positive benefit ... is that a wider range of publications should be made available for the same expenditure.

Martin and Wolf (25) provide an excellent overview of the many issues around this topic whilst also providing insights into the overall view of planning a library resource budget. Other readings are listed in Chapter 8.

6. Software packages

Financial packages are available in many forms ranging from the mainframe systems used by companies to process their financial data to 'simple' spreadsheets which can be used to create applications for the information unit alone. Available packages range from fully integrated enterprise management systems, such as SAP™, via full accounting systems to simple bookkeeping systems. Packages can cost anything from a few tens to many tens of thousands of pounds, depending on their complexity, number of users and target audience. Packages are available to handle any, or all, of the functions listed below.

- general, nominal, purchase and sales ledgers
- profit and loss accounting and management information
- billing and accounts receivable
- payment and accounts payable
- payroll management
- employee benefits
- budget management and forecasting
- financial reporting
- fund analysis
- capital assets and depreciation
- job costing systems
- subscription and deposit account management
- enterprise resource management

A variety of sources are available which list software including: the hardcopy *Software Users Year book (26)* and a number of online databases, including *Softbase: Reviews, Companies and Products*.

6.1 Spreadsheets

Spreadsheets are computer packages that provide the electronic means to enter, perform calculations on and store data. The various examples of budgets and financial reports used as illustrations in this volume have all been prepared using a spreadsheet package and illustrate the basic use of the technology.

It must be stressed that spreadsheets do not undertake any function that cannot be achieved using paper and pencil. Spreadsheets, however, ease the clerical work involved in financial management by their ability:

- to speed the working process
- to allow projections to be revised where errors and omissions are discovered
- to allow the application of 'what if' scenarios – the development of a series of projections using different assumptions
- to simplify the analysis and calculation of variances.

In short, spreadsheets have become an extremely powerful management tool.

Spreadsheet packages provide a variety of functions that make certain aspects of financial management easier to perform. Financial modelling and budgeting is one such area and with modern spreadsheet packages permitting the construction of multi-page documents it is now possible to perform on a personal computer tasks which 10 years ago required sophisticated accounting packages running on mainframe computers.

All modern spreadsheet packages also provide a facility for the graphical presentation of data. It has long been recognised that graphs (or charts) can provide a powerful means of presenting complex data. In financial management the presentation of figures in graphical form can ensure that trends can be seen without the need to compare complex tables. Figure 9 illustrates this principle.

Within the United Kingdom the most commonly used spreadsheet packages are Lotus 1-2-3™ and Microsoft Excel™.

It is not the role of this volume to teach spreadsheet technique; Secrett (27) provides a recent text, one of many available, on the use of spreadsheets in general financial management. However, I have found from personal experience that the last publication you should read to learn about a particular package is the accompanying software manual. Having said that, they *are* useful when you have a specific problem to solve. Furthermore do not assume that the presence of online help automatically removes the need to use manuals!

The easiest ways to gain familiarisation with a spreadsheet are either to use the tutorial that comes with the package or else simply to start with a blank screen and construct a simple spreadsheet using

Year ended March 31st	1983	1984	1985	1986	1987	1988	1989	1990	1991	1992	1993	1994
Operating Activity	-2764	1023	9226	2456	-1343	-4916	-14046	4357	-15705	-242	-7063	10451
Investment Income	5440	5461	5213	7444	6634	6092	5635	6407	7310	5019	4236	4441
Deficit/surplus	2676	6484	14439	9900	5291	1176	-8411	10764	-8395	4777	-2827	14892
Turnover	92409	108011	123402	168919	177354	192140	229267	453628	455073	477222	477343	414757

XYZ Company Financial Results (000s)

Figure 9: Comparison of Tablular and Graphical Presentation

information that is available in your information unit. It is also worth remembering, before entering a state of panic with a particular problem, that a lot of information is presented on the screen to explain what is going on. *Don't just look at the screen, **READ IT!***

6.2 Information unit use of spreadsheets

The need to ensure that up-to-date financial information is available to the information manager has already been noted. Most information units will be part of organisations that have management accounting and finance groups. However, any information received from these sources will naturally be out of date. Central financial units generally provide reports monthly, *often in the middle* of the following month reflecting expenditure situations at the end of the previous month. This does not provide the basic information needed for accurate financial management.

The automated acquisitions systems and similar systems used in many libraries will provide accurate and timely financial management information for the information unit. These fully integrated systems will be able to report and analyse financial information by, amongst other parameters, internal account code, vendor, actual and commitment expenditure.

Of course not all information units will have sophisticated systems. With the advances in spreadsheet software it is, however, easy for any information officer to maintain sophisticated financial management information systems internally to the library.

In addition to the specific uses discussed below, it would of course be possible for an information unit to devise spreadsheet applications to cover all its financial software needs.

6.2.1 Budgeting and budget reporting

Although management will control the budgeting process, spreadsheets can also have their use during the initial processes undertaken in the information unit. Secrett (27), who is highlighting spreadsheet usage for small/medium business, provides practical guidance as to how spreadsheets can be used for monitoring actual expenditure against budget, recommending a combination of paper copy (where manual methods must be adopted for the calculation of variances) and key copy (where multiple copies of the budget spreadsheet are used and the spreadsheet is used to calculate the variances).

6.2.2 Financial (transaction) reporting

In all organisations the corporate finance department will provide financial information to the information manager. However, the difficulty with this information is that it will only be provided at the level of analysis required by the corporate budget. Information managers should of course work with their financial colleagues to ensure that where systems, such as SAP™, are used at a corporate level that the needs of the information unit are taken into account.

Where this is not possible and the need for more detailed information is required, then the information unit should implement its own systems.

In 1995 Amerada Hess Limited reported all expenditure on publications at the information unit level by the three detail codes that were used for corporate budgeting purposes, where all expenditure on publications is recorded against the Hess Information Centre. At the corporate level the company does not require further analysis. The information unit naturally required a more detailed analysis, at the departmental level, which indicated on what resources were actually spent.

Furthermore, information unit management, as indicated in Chapter 4, must have an accurate analysis of commitment expense both on the basis of individual orders raised during the financial year and also on recurrent orders such as 'standing orders for monographs' and the journals budget. If your journals budget is mainly paid at the end of the financial year it is essential that interim financial statements generated during the year indicate the appropriate level of commitment expenditure involved.

To provide the level of day to day information required for management purposes within the Hess Information Centre a series of eight spreadsheets, compiled as an EXCEL5™ workbook, were used to record all expenditure both actual and commitment, as paperwork was raised for purchase or authorised for payment. A full description is given in Appendix B.

Apart from these relatively complex spreadsheets, which could be replaced by data derived from automated acquisitions systems, the same principles can be used to manage many simpler financial matters including:

- calculations and analysis during costing processes
- recording movements in deposit accounts
- petty cash management.

7. Organisations

Various professional and commercial bodies are available to provide assistance to information workers seeking help in the financial management area. Address details were verified in late February 2003.

7.1 Information oriented organisations

ASLIB (Association for Information Management)

Temple Chambers

3-7 Temple Avenue

London EC4Y 0HP

Tel: +44 (0) 20 7583 8900

Fax: +44 (0) 20 7583 8401

www.aslib.com

Chartered Institute of Library and Information

Professionals (Cilip)

7 Ridgmount Street

London WC1E 7AE

Tel: +44 (0) 20 7255 0500

Fax: +44 (0) 20 7255 0501

www.cilip.org.uk

Industrial Society Bookings Unit

Freepost NM4380

Birmingham B15 1BR

Tel: +44 (0) 121 452 1030

TFPL Ltd

17-18 Britton Street

London   EC1M 5TL

Tel: +44 (0) 20 7251 5522

Fax: +44 (0) 20 7251 8318

www.tfpl.com

Groups and branches of these national organisations often run short courses.

7.2 Accountancy oriented organisations

Association of Accounting Technicians

154 Clerkenwell Road

London EC1R 5AD

Tel: +44 (0) 20 7837 8600

Fax: +44 (0) 20 7837 6970

Email: *aat@aat.org.uk*

www.aat.co.uk

Chartered Institute of Management Accountants

26 Chapter Street

London SW1P 4NP

Tel: +44 (0) 20 7663 5441

Fax: +44 (0) 20 7663 5442

www.cimaglobal.com

The Chartered Institute of Public Finance and Accountancy

3 Robert Street

London WC2N 6RL

Tel: +44 (0) 20 7543 5600

Fax: +44 (0) 20 7543 5700

www.cipfa.org.uk

Institute of Chartered Accountants in England & Wales

PO Box 433

Charted Accountants Hall

Moorgate Place

London EC2P 2BJ

Tel: +44 (0) 20 7920 8100

Fax: +44 (0) 20 7920 0547

www.icaew.co.uk

Institute of Chartered Accountants of Scotland

CA House,

21 Haymarket Yards,

Edinburgh EH12 5BH

Tel: +44 (0) 131 347 0100

Fax: +44 (0) 131 347 0105

www.icas.org.uk

Institute of Chartered Accountants in Ireland

87 – 89 Pembroke Road

Ballsbridge

Dublin 4

Republic of Ireland

Tel: +353-1-637 7200

Fax: +353-1-668 0842

www.icai.ie/Welcome.html

8. Further reading

8.1 References

1. Hewgill, J.C.R. 'Management accounting and library activities', *Aslib Proceedings*, 29(9), (1977), pp 304–9.

2. Alley, B. and Cargill, J. *Keeping Track of What you Spend: The Librarian's Guide to Simple Bookkeeping* (Phoenix: Oryx Press, 1982).

3a. Roberts, S.A. *Cost Management for Library and Information Services* (London: Butterworths, 1985).

3b. Roberts, S.A. *Financial and Cost Management for Libraries and Information Services* (London: Butterworths, 1997).

4. Warner, A.S. *Owning your Numbers: an Introduction to Budgeting for Special Libraries* (Washington: Special Libraries Association, 1992).

5. *Oxford English Dictionary, Compact Edition*, Volume 1 A–O (London: Book Club Associates, 1979).

6. *Oxford English Dictionary, Compact Edition*, Volume 3 – A supplement to the Oxford English Dictionary volumes I–IV (Oxford: Oxford University Press, 1987).

7. McElroy, A.R. ed *College Librarianship* (London: Library Association, 1984) (Introduction).

8. Stoffle, C. 'Funding and creativity, Part 1: Funding', *Bulletin of ASIS*, 17, (1990/1, December/January), pp 16–18.

9. Koenig, M.E.D. *Budgeting Techniques for Libraries and Information Centres* (New York: Special Libraries Association, 1980).

10. Talbot, R.J. 'Financing the academic library', in Galvin, T. and Lynch, B. eds. *New Directions in Higher Education: Priorities for Academic Libraries*, no. 39 (San Francisco: Jossey-Bass, 1972) pp 35-44.

11. Corrall, S. *Strategic Planning for Library and Information Services*, Aslib Know How Guide (London: Aslib, 1994).

12. Lovecy, I. 'Budgeting in university libraries', *Serials*, 5(1), (1992), pp 43–51.

13. Black, W.K. 'The budget as a planning tool', *Journal of Library Administration*, 18(3/4), (1993), pp 171–88.

14. Robinson, B.M. and Robinson, S. 'Strategic planning and program budgeting for libraries', *Library Trends*, 42(3), (1994), pp 420-47.

15. Stewart, J.D. 'The determination of management objectives, priorities, and techniques of output measurement for the library service', in *Planning, Programming, Budgeting Systems in Libraries: a Symposium* (Library Association – East Midlands Branch, 1975).

16a. Pearson, D. and Yates-Mercer, P.A. 'Charging policies and practice in corporate information units in the UK. Part 1: To charge or not to charge', *Journal of Information Science*, 18(1), (1992), pp 11–25.

16b. Pearson, D. and Yates-Mercer, P.A. 'Charging policies and practice in corporate information units in the UK. Part 2: How to charge', *Journal of Information Science*, 18(2), (1992), pp 127–37.

17. Webb, S. *Making a Charge for Library and Information Services*, Aslib Know How Guide (London: Aslib, 1994).

18. McLean, N. 'A bigger slice: cost justification for library and information services', *Aslib Proceedings*, 39(10), (1987), pp 293–7.

19. Office of Arts and Libraries (OAL) *Keys to Success: Performance Indicators for Public Libraries.* A manual of performance measures and indicators developed by King Research Limited. Library Information Series, no. 18 (London: HMSO, 1990).

20. Clements, D.W.G. 'The costing of library systems', *Aslib Proceedings*, 27(3), (1975), pp 98–111.

21a. Beecher, J.W. et al. 'Use of random alarm mechanisms for analyzing professional and support staff in science libraries. Part 1: "Methodology", *Library Research*, 4(2), (1982), pp 137–46.

21b. Beecher, J.W. et al. 'Use of random alarm mechanisms for analyzing professional and support staff in science libraries. Part 2: "Data analysis and discussion", *Library Research*, 4(2), (1982), pp 147–61.

22. Mitchell, B.J., Tanis, N.E. and Jaffe, J. *Cost Analysis of Library Functions: a Total System Approach.* Foundations in Library & Information Science, vol. 6 (Greenwich, Conn: JAI Press, 1978). Pp 61–8 provide a detailed, although organisation specific, description of library tasks.

23. Montgomery, C.H. and Sparks, J. 'Framework for assessing the impact of an electronic journal

collection on library costs and staffing patterns' (March 2000). *www.si.umich.edu/PEAK-2000/ montgomery.pdf*

24. Friend, F. J. 'Changing the financial model for libraries', *Serials,* 12 (1), (1999), pp 7–11

25. Martin, M.S. and Wolf, M. *Budgeting for Information Access 2nd Ed.* (Washington: American Library Association. 1998).

26. *Software Users Year Book* ed. A. Maher (London: VNU Publishing, 1994 and later editions).

27. Secrett, M. *Mastering Spreadsheet Budgets and Forecasts: a Practical Guide* (London: Pitman in association with Institute of Management, 1993).

8.2 Bibliography

The list of readings presented here is but a small part of the literature on financial management published in the library and information field. I hope that readers will find it useful. Since the publication of the first edition the literature has grown as the profession has seen the need to be more proactive in its use of financial management principles.

Abell, A. 'Costing and charging – tools for the job', *Outlook on Research Libraries*, 11(4), (1989), pp 1–4.

Abels, E.G. and Lunin, L.F. eds. 'Perspectives on costs and pricing of library and information services in transition', *JASIS*, 47(3), (1996), pp 207–46 [Set of four papers].

Akeroyd, J. 'Costing, pricing and financial control', in *The Information Business – issues for the 1990s*

(Hatfield: Hertis Information & Research, 1991) pp 34–45.

Akeroyd, J. 'Costing and pricing information: the bottom line', *Aslib Proceedings*, 42(2/3), (1991), pp 87–92.

Allen, F.R. 'Materials budgets in the electronic age: a survey of academic libraries', *College & Research Libraries*, 57(2), (1996), pp 133–43.

Allen, G.G. and Tat, L.C. 'The development of an objective budget allocation procedure for academic library acquisitions', *Libri*, 37(3),(1987), pp 211–21.

Aren, L.J. and Webreck, S.J. 'Costing library operations - a bibliography', *Collection Building*, 8(3), (1987), pp 23-8.

Badenoch, D. et al. 'The value of information', in Feeney, M. and Grieves, M. eds. *The Value and Impact of Information* British Library Research Information Policy Issues (East Grinstead: Bowker Saur, 1994) pp 9–77.

Barnes, M.E. 'Managing with technology: automating budgeting from acquisitions', *The Bottom Line*, 10(2), (1997), pp 65–73.

Barnes, R.M. *Motion and Time Study Design and Measurement of Work* (New York: Wiley, 1968).

Bentley, S. and LaGuardia, C. 'Bell, book, and budget: quenching the costs of computerized library resources', *Microcomputers for Information Management*, 11(1), (1994), pp 13–22.

Bjarno, H. 'Cost finding and performance measures in ILL management', *Interlending and Document Supply*, 22(2), (1994), pp 8–11.

Blagden, J. 'Achieving beneficial outcomes: the key priorities for information managers', in Dossett, P. ed. *Handbook of Special Librarianship and Information Work* 6th ed. (London: Aslib, 1992).

Blick, A.R. 'Evaluating an in-house or bought-in service', *Aslib Proceedings*, 29(9), (1977), pp 310–9.

Brockman, J.R. *The Costs of Academic Libraries: an Econometric Interpretation*. Western Library Studies, vol. 4 (Perth (WA), Curtin University of Technology, 1988). (Includes a summary of published library cost and production figures.)

Brophy, P. 'Budgeting in academic libraries: the polytechnic perspective', *Serials*, 5(1), (1992), pp 35–41.

Carpenter, K.H. 'Forecasting expenditures for library materials: approaches and techniques', *Acquisitions Librarian*, no 2, (1989), pp 31–48.

Catchside, P. 'Budgeting in real life' *Serials*, 5(1), (1992) pp 53–6.

Chen, C. C. *Zero Based Budgeting in Library Management* (New York: Oryx Press, 1980).

Cline, G.S. 'Budgeting for reference services in the academic library: a tutorial', *Reference Librarian*, 19, (1987), pp 53–73.

Cook, J. 'Financing a library/information service by operating a cost recovery system', *Aslib Proceedings*, 24(6), (1972), pp 342–9.

Cooper, R. 'The rise of activity-based costing. Part 1 – What is an activity-based cost system?', *Journal of Cost Management*, (1988) Summer, pp 45–54.

Cooper, R. 'The rise of activity-based costing. Part 2 – When do I need an activity-based cost system?', *Journal of Cost Management*, (1988) Fall, pp 41–8.

Cooper, R. 'Implementing an activity-based cost system' *Journal of Cost Management*, (1990), Spring, pp 33–42.

Cornella, A. 'Cost, value and price in fee-based information services' (1992). *www.infonomics.net/cornella/afid.html*

Cropley, J. 'Budgeting', in Wood, L. ed. *Resource Allocation in Industrial and Commercial Libraries: Optimising New Technology and New Services* (1988), pp 53–59.

Cropley, J. 'Budgeting in special libraries', *Serials*, 5(1), (1992), pp 58-61.

Danilenko, G. 'Activity based costing for services: the Corporate Information Centre', *Special Libraries*, (1994), Winter, pp 24–9.

Daubert, M.J. *Financial Management for Small and Medium-sized Libraries* (Chicago: American Library Association, 1993).

Daubert, M.J. *Money Talk: Accounting Fundamentals for Special Libraries. A Self-study Program* (Washington: Special Libraries Association, 1995).

Daubert, M.J. *Control of Administration and Financial Operations in Special Libraries. A Self-study Program* (Washington: Special Libraries Association, 1996).

Dunn, J.A. and Martin, M.S. 'The whole cost of libraries', *Library Trends*, 42(3), (1994), pp 564–78.

Fogo, T. and Bartlett, G. *Financial Management for Librarians: Managing Resources* (Open learning for library staff). (Newcastle upon Tyne: Northern Training Group/Scottish Council for Educational Technology, 1993).

Fraley, R.A. and Katz, B. eds. 'Finance, budget and management for reference services', *Reference Librarian*, 19, (1987), (complete issue with a number of papers of relevance to financial management).

Griffin, M. 'Putting a price on information: practice illustrating a basic principle', *Aslib Proceedings*, 32(1), (1980), pp 26–34.

Grotenhuis, A. 'The user pays: cost billing in a company library', *Special Libraries*, 86(2), (1995) pp 110–16.

Gyeszley, S.D. 'Electronic or paper journals? Budgetary, collection development and user satisfaction questions', *Collection Building*, 20(1), (2001), pp 5–10.

Hayes, R.M. 'The economics of digital libraries.' *www.usp.br/sibi/economics.html*

Hayes, S. and Brown, D. 'The library as a business: mapping the pervasiveness of financial relationships in today's library', *Library Trends*, 42(3), (1994), pp 404–19.

Heery, M. 'Winning resources', *The Bottom Line*, 12(2), (1999), pp 57-67.

Innes, J. and Mitchell, F. *Activity Based Costing. A Review with Case Studies* (London: CIMA (Chartered Institute of Management Accountants), 1990).

Innes, J. and Mitchell, F. *A Practical Guide to Activity Based Costing* (London: Kogan Page, 1998).

Jones, L. and Nicholas, D. 'Costing medical libraries: the feasibility of functional cost analysis', *Health Libraries Review*, 10(4), (1993), pp 169–201.

Kantor, P.B. 'Library cost analysis', *Library Trends*, 38(2), (1989), pp 171–88.

Kantor, P.B., Saracevic, T. and D'Esposito-Wachtman, J. *Studying the Cost and Value of Library Services: Final Report* (New Brunswick, NJ: Rutgers State University of New Jersey, School of Communication, Information and Library Studies, Alexandria Project Laboratory 1995). Technical Report APLAB/94-3/1,2,3,4.

Kingma, B.R. *The economics of Information: a Guide to Economic and Cost-benefit Analysis for Information Professionals* (Englewood, CO: Libraries Unlimited, 1996).

Koenig, M.E.D. and Alperin, V. 'ZBB and PPBS: what's left now that the trendiness has gone?' *Drexel Library Quarterly*, 21(3), (1987), pp 19–38.

Martin, M.S. ed. 'Library Finance: New needs, new models' *Library Trends*, 42(3), (1994), pp 369–584 (complete issue).

Martin, M.S. *Academic Library Budgets* Greenwich Conn. (London: JAI Press Inc, 1994).

Martin, M.S. *Collection Development and Finance: a Guide to Strategic Library-materials Budgeting* (Washington: American Library Association, 1995).

McPherson, P.K. 'Accounting for the value of information', *Aslib Proceedings*, 46(9), (1994), pp 203–15

Miekle, L. 'Cost finding: why it is important' *Public Libraries*, 29(5), (1990), pp 282–8.

Millership, J.J.G. 'The librarian as financial manager', papers presented at the CoFHE Annual Study Conference, 1989 (London: CoFHE, 1989). (Includes three case studies: 'Finance and the Freedom to Manage'.)

Morris, D.E. 'Staff time and costs for cataloguing' *Library Resources and Technical Services*, 36(1), (1992) pp 79–95.

Niles, J.F. 'How I learned to stop worrying and love the budget', *Acquisitions Librarian*, 2, (1989), pp 69–83.

O'Donovan, K. ed. 'Costing library services - towards a model for the NHS'. Proceedings of a seminar and workshop held at the University of Newcastle upon Tyne 13 December 1990. *Health Libraries Review*, 8(3), (1991), pp 120–41.

Office of Arts and Libraries (OAL). *A Costing System for Public Libraries*. A model system developed by Cipfa Services Ltd in conjunction with the Institute of Public Finance Ltd. Library Information Series no. 17 (London: HMSO, 1987).

Pantry, S. & Roberts, S. *The Handbook of Financial Management for Information Professionals*, in press (London: Library Association 1995).

Planning, Programming, Budgeting Systems in Libraries: a Symposium. ([SL]: Library Association – East Midlands Branch, 1975).

Prentice, A. ed. *Financial Planning for Libraries 2nd ed.* (Metuchen NJ: Scarecrow Press,1996).

Prentice, A. ed. 'Budgeting and accounting', *Drexel Library Quarterly,* 21(3) (complete issue), (1985). (Note papers have a copyright date of 1987.)

Roberts, S.A. *Costing and the Economics of Library and Information Services* Aslib Reader Series no 5 (London: Aslib, 1984). (Includes many of the standard papers on costing and management accounting for libraries.)

Rosenberg, P. *Cost Finding for Public Libraries: a Manager's Handbook* (Chicago: American Library Association, 1985).

Rounds, R.S. *Budgeting Practices for Librarians,* 2nd ed. (Chicago: American Library Association, 1994).

Satin, S. 'Negotiating: from first contact to final contract', Searcher, 9(6), (2001), pp 50–4. Also at *www.infotoday.com/searcher/jun01/satin.htm*

Schneider, K.G. 'The Tao of internet costs', *The Bottom Line*, 11(2), (1998), pp 52–64.

Sellen, B.C. and Turock, B.J. *The Bottom Line Reader: a Financial Handbook for Librarians.* (New York: Neal-Schuman, 1990). (A collection of readings.)

Shepherd, C. 'Assessing intranet cost-benefits'. *www.fastrak-consulting.co.uk/tactix/Features/costbens/ costbens.htm*

Siess, J. 'The dreaded "B" word: budgeting and financial matters', *One-Person Library*, 17(2), (2000), pp 1–5.

Smith, G. S. *Accounting for Librarians and Other Not-for-profit Managers* (Chicago: American Library Association, 1983). (Given its American provenance it is not surprising that the terminology relates to American practice. The principles can easily be applied to the United Kingdom.)

Snyder, H. and Davenport, E. *Costing and Pricing in the Digital Age: a Practical Guide for Information Services* (New York: Neal-Schuman, 1997).

Snyder, H. amd Davenport, E. 'What does it really cost? Allocating indirect costs', *The Bottom Line*, 10(4), (1997), pp 158–64.

Stephens, A. 'The application of life cycle costing in libraries: a case study based on acquisition and retention of library materials in the British Library', *IFLA Journal*, 20(2), (1994), pp 130–40.

Tebbetts, D.R. 'The costs of information technology and the electronic library', *The Electronic Library*, 18(2), (2000), pp 127–36.

Turock, B.J. and Pedolsky, A. *Creating a Financial Plan: a How-to-do-it Manual for Librarians* (New York: Neal-Schuman, 1992).

Warner, A.S. 'Money matters: six hints for information managers', *Online*, (1991), March, pp 26–8.

Warner, A.S. *Budgeting: a How-to-do-it Manual for Librarians* (New York: Neal-Schuman, 1998).

Weingand, D.E. 'What do products/services cost? How do we know?' *Library Trends* 43(3), (1995), pp 401–8.

Whelan, H. 'In-house charging for information', in *The Information Business – Issues for the 1990s* (Hatfield: Hertis Information & Research, 1991), pp 46–57.

White, G.W. and Crawford, G.A. 'Cost-benefit analyses of electronic information: a case study', *College & Research Libraries*, (1998), pp 503–10.

Woodsworth, A. and Williams, J.F. *Managing the Economics of Owning, Leasing and Contracting out Information Services* (London: Ashgate, 1993) (especially Chapter 7 – Costs and charging strategies).

Young, H.C. *Planning, Programming, Budgeting Systems in Academic Libraries* (Detroit: Gale, 1976).

In addition to the references quoted there are a number of journals that often have articles on accounting and other aspects of financial management:

Accountancy

Accounting Review

Administrative Management

Bottom Line (The)

Fee for Service

Harvard Business Review

Library Acquisitions

Library Resources and Technical Services

Management Accounting

Management Review

Management Science

Managerial Planning

Special Libraries

Wilson Library Bulletin

The number of general textbooks dealing with accounting and financial management is vast and wide-ranging. Quick searches using *www.amazon.co.uk* (6 September 2001) produced 406 titles in response to the word 'spreadsheet' and 5,174 in response to 'finance and management'. The problem with most of these titles is that they are *generally aimed at students and practitioners of accounting and related subjects* and library and information staff should be aware that since many titles go into considerable technical and specialist detail they may not be suitable for use at a generalist level.

The various professional accountancy bodies publish books aimed at their members whilst commercial publishers including Pitman and DPP also publish a range of suitable books.

Appendix A. Example budget submission

Part of the actual budget, as presented, for XYZ Oil Company's Exploration Division Library Service for fiscal year 1984. (Although this example is dated 1984, the principles still apply.) The library was only concerned with published materials.

The overall budget submission for 1984 comprised five parts.

- revenue budget schedules as presented to the corporate management team
- acquisitions with detailed discussion on a line by line basis for consideration at departmental level
- training proposals discussion for consideration at departmental level
- cost centre overheads discussion for consideration at departmental level
- capital budget schedules as presented to the corporate management team.

Selective extracts only from Acquisitions section:

Fund	1983	Proposed 1984
Books	15000	20000
Serials	15000	19500
Bibliographic publications	8550	9500
General maps	7050	8000
Information sciences	600	600
Inter-library loans	2000	2350
Online services (general)	6500	8500
Online services (SDI)	1100	1500
Consultancy reports	25000	28000
Special reports	7000	7000
Reprints	1250	1500
Miscellaneous	1500	1500
TOTAL ROUTINE	90550	107950
Special map collection	16727	20000
Consultants microfiche	nil	12500
TOTAL BUDGET REQUEST	107277	140450

Within the budget submission each fund was presented in the form:

1984 ACQUISITIONS BUDGET
FUND : [Name of account]   1983 Budget
Proposed 1984 Budget
Justification

Book fund: The original 1983 budget included a provision of just over £10,000 for books. Continuing increases in demand especially from the Laboratory and International Exploration have resulted in the book fund expending over £7,000 in the first six months of the current year, with no sign of a reduction in demand, hence the budgetary revision to £15,000 in July. With book prices rising at a conservative rate of 15 per cent per annum, compounded by the comparative weakness in sterling (in 1982 some 35 per cent of our books were paid in foreign currencies and many of those paid in sterling are based on conversion rates) together with increasing demands from our major user groups we feel that a budget of £20,000 is not unrealistic.

Serials fund: Although presented as a single line in the schedule a detailed justification in the four accounting groups (below) is presented on succeeding pages:

Renewals	£14,500
New titles	£2,000
Back issues	£2,500
Binding	£500

It must be stressed that serials, although a continuing and on-going commitment, are probably the most important single acquisition within the library budget. Cuts in the serials budget can only be countered by large increases in the interlibrary loans budget with consequent loss of service to our readers. When all historic factors are eliminated, for instance the extremely low price for *Petroleum Abstracts* in the early years, our total expenditure on serials (excluding PA), including back issues, has risen from £5,000 in 1978 to £12,000 in 1982, estimated £15,000 in 1983 and a proposal of £19,500 in 1984. This 290 per cent increase represents an increase of about 21.5 per cent compounded per annum. With actual periodical charges rising on average by 15 per cent, the divisional staff numbers increasing by some 200 plus since 1978 and considering that our back issue programme did not really exist in earnest until 1980, I do not consider this to be excessive.

Special map collection: The provision of commercially published maps that are relevant to the needs of explorers is an area of library activity that requires considerable resources in three significant areas: finance, accommodation and staff. Following comments from the General Manager of Exploration in 1982, provision, initially of £20,000, reduced to just over £16,000 in July 1983, was made in the 1983 budget for the initial development of a world-wide collection of relevant earth science map coverage from around the world. We would request provision of an additional £20,000 in 1984 to allow for the continued development of this collection.

Appendix B. Use of spreadsheets for financial management: the example of the Hess Information Centre

Figure 10 illustrates:

- the overall summary sheet presented in *formulae* format
- the headings for each of the other sheets with any calculations, again, presented in *formulae* format.

The rest of this appendix comprises the internal working instructions, effective in fiscal year 1995, and provides an example of what can be done within an information unit where corporate level systems do not provide the required level of management information needed.

The financial information for Hess Information Centre (Library) will be retained in yearly EXCEL5™ workbooks named BUDGETnn, e.g. BUDGET95. Workbooks are held on the information centre shared drive in directory \libfin\ which is write protected with a read-only recommendation. The password will be issued on a need to know basis.

The workbook comprises a:

	A	B	C	D	E	F	G	H	I
1	Summary Table								
3	Document Type	Code	Budget	Actuals	Committed	Total	Free Balance		
5	Books	96F063A	Budget A			=SUM(C5:F6)	=SUM(C5:F6)		
6	Journals	96F063B	Budget B			=SUM(C7:F7)	=SUM(C7:F7)		
7	Miscellaneous	96F063X	Budget C			=SUM(C8:F8)	=SUM(C8:F8)		
10	Totals	=SUM(C5:C8)	=SUM(C5:C8)	=SUM(D5:D8)	=SUM(E5:E8)	=SUM(C10:F10)	=SUM(C10:F10)		
12	Online Services	96F063X	Budget D						
13					Unallowable	=D13	=C13+F13		
17	Book Fund								
18	DATE	INDENT	AHL Ref L	INVOICE NO	SUPPLIER	User Cost Centre	96F063A	Estimated £	Invoice Signed Off
19						Total	=SUM(G25:G1016)	=SUM(H25:H1016)	
24	Periodicals								
25	DATE	AHL Ref L	INVOICE NO	SUPPLIER	96F063B	Estimated £	Invoiced Signed Off		
26		n/a	Estimates		=SUM(F26:F1024)	=SUM(F26:F1024)			
27	1995			Dateacons					
30	Miscellaneous								
32	DATE	INDENT	AHL Ref L	INVOICE NO	SUPPLIER	User Cost Centre	96F063X	Estimated £	Invoice Signed Off
34						Totals	=SUM(G36:G1031)	=SUM(H36:H1031)	
37	Standing Orders								
39	Title	Supplier	Copies	Order Number	Notes	1995 Received	Estimated	Actual	
40	Totals						=SUM(G34:G1042)		
42	Subscriptions								
44		Dept	Due	1995-96 Price	1995-96 Price	AHL Ref			
45				Estimates	Actuals				
46				=SUM(D46:D101)	=SUM(E46:E101)				
47	Totals				=SUM(E46:E1101)				
50	Newspapers								
51	User	User Cost Centre	1995 Total	Month	Oct	Nov	Dec	Jan	
52			=SUM(D52:D53)	Total					
53			=SUM(D54:D54)	Estimated	50XX	50368	=F53	=F53	
54				AHL Ref	672XON	242XON			
55				Inv No	34696	34711			
57				Approved					
61	Total	=SUM(C64:I64)	Vendor 1	Vendor 2	Vendor 3	Vendor 4	Vendor 5	Vendor 6	Vendor 7
64	Date (Signed)	Host Totals >>> Payment Ref >	=SUM(C56:C184)	=SUM(D56:D184)	=SUM(E56:E185)	=SUM(F56:F184)	=SUM(G56:G184)	=SUM(H56:H194)	=SUM(I56:I194)

- summary sheet
- book fund sheet
- journals fund sheet
- miscellaneous fund sheet
- standing orders sheet
- newspapers sheet
- periodical listing and charges sheet.

In addition a separate sheet, the Online Information Retrieval sheet, is used to record all invoice transactions for these services and is held in this workbook to keep all budget documents together.

Summary accounts page: approved budget figures are entered here and linked to the other sheets to provide the totals. The free balance (uncommitted balance) is calculated automatically on this sheet. In addition summary figures for online expenditure are also noted here.

Book fund: after the sheet title line the first line relates to the estimated commitment for standing orders for regular publications. This total is derived from a linkage to the standing orders sheet and will decline during the year as orders are actually paid for – invoices are entered in this sheet. For further details see section below on standing orders.

The next several lines relate to publications ordered before 1 January 1995 that had not been invoiced at the year-end – these are simply derived by copying the appropriate lines from the earlier year's finance pages.

All book orders are entered into this spreadsheet at the time of commitment (ordering) thereby allowing management to be aware of the totals committed.

The line format for all entries is as follows.

Date	The date of the order, or of invoice in case of standing orders
Indent	Number of indent or local purchase order as applicable. For standing order invoices use the abbreviation SO
AHL Ref. L	AHLs invoice reference (numbers only)
Invoice	Supplier's invoice reference
Supplier	Name of supplier (please be consistent); major suppliers are listed in the appendix to this procedure.
User cost centre	The detail code, e.g. PHICX, of the user department for whom the publication is purchased. For books purchased by HIC for the general good use ZHIC.
88F053A	The actual amount of the invoice *excluding VAT.*
Estimated	Estimated cost of publications at time of ordering. This field MUST be completed at time of order. The field is to be cleared once an invoiced total has been entered in 88F053A.
88F053A/Estimated	Only ONE of these to be completed at any one time
Invoiced signed	Date of signature by library staff of invoice apron

Journals fund: after the sheet title the first line relates to the estimated commitment for serials to be purchased during the year, mainly from Dawson Periodicals. This total is derived from a linkage to the periodicals listing and charges sheet and will decline during the year as orders are actually paid for – invoices are entered in this sheet. For further details see section below on periodicals.

Unlike books there is no carry forward for publications ordered before 1 January 1995 that had not been invoiced at the year-end.

Invoices are entered into this spreadsheet at the time of approval; commitment accounting is derived from the periodical listing file.

The line format for all entries is as follows.

Date	Date of signature by library staff of invoice apron
AHL Ref. L	AHLs invoice reference (numbers only)
Invoice	Supplier's invoice reference
Supplier	Name of supplier (please be consistent); major suppliers are listed in the appendix to this procedure.
88F053B	The actual amount of the invoice *excluding VAT.*
Estimated	Estimated cost of publications at time of ordering. This figure is derived by linkage from the periodical listing file and is only entered once.

Miscellaneous fund: items charged to this account relate to press cuttings, newspapers and other publications not charged to books and journals.

An approximate commitment for press cuttings and newspapers is calculated at the start of the year for inclusion in this section of the spreadsheet. Full cost centre accounting for newspapers is provided in the newspapers sheet – where invoices for that supplier are entered in full.

Invoices are normally entered into this spreadsheet at the time of approval.

The line format for all entries is as follows.

Date	The date of the order, or of invoice in case of standing orders
Indent	Number of indent or local purchase order as applicable. For standing order invoices when entered use the abbreviation SO.
AHL Ref. L	AHLs invoice reference (numbers only)
Invoice	Supplier's invoice reference
Supplier	Name of supplier (please be consistent); major suppliers are listed in the appendix to this procedure.
User cost centre	The detail code, e.g. PHICX, of the user department for whom the publication is purchased. For books purchased by HIC for the general good use ZHIC.
88F053X	The actual amount of the invoice *excluding VAT*.
Estimated	Estimated cost of publications at time of ordering. This figure is derived by linkage from the periodicals listing file.
Invoiced signed	Date of signature by library staff of invoice apron

Standing orders

The standing orders file provides commitment control for the costs of those monographic publications that are supplied with each new edition, or on other standing order principles.

Invoice details for documents received on standing order should be entered into the books sheet.

Title	The title of the document or service received on standing order
S(upplier)	W=Dawsons D=Direct from publisher B=Butterworths H=HMSO
C(opies)	Number of copies ordered
Order	Order number where known
Notes	Relevant order information
1995 Received	Date 1995 edition(s) received
Estimated	1994 price or best estimate; this field is cleared (or reduced) where charges are incurred.
Actual	Actual price invoiced in 1995. Note that these figures will become the basis for the estimated prices used in 1996

Periodical listing and charges

This table provides a comprehensive listing of periodical titles received by the HIC (Library) together with indicative prices for commitment purposes and provision for entry of actual prices to allow review of cost centre expenditure.

Details of invoices are included in the periodicals sheet, at an invoice level.

Title	Journal title
Dept	Cost centre for which purchased or most relevant. Use ZHIC for those titles purchased for the general good of the company.
Due	Approximate renewal date
1995–96 Price estimate	Best estimate of next renewal price
1995–96 Price actual	Actual invoiced price for renewal during 1995
1995–96 Estimate/Actual	Only ONE of these to be completed at any one time
AHL Ref.	AHL L Number.

Newspapers

This file can be used for any AHL specified supplier.

Each payment month is represented by a column, (letters F through Q). Invoicing information is added to rows 4 through 6 for each column as billings are paid.

Row 1	Title row
Row 2 (columns F>Q)	Calculated total for month
Row 3 (columns G>Q)	Estimated amount, based on previous month's billings. This field should be cleared after receipt of invoice.
Row 4 AHL Ref.	Accounts payable ref. number Lnnnnn
Row 5 invoice no.	Supplier invoice number
Row 6 approved	Date of approval of invoice

The billing detail is specified in the rest of the spreadsheet.

Column A/B	User name and initials
Column C	User cost centre
Column D	Calculated field – total billings
Column E	Blank
Columns F through Q	Actual amounts paid for each user receiving newspapers etc.
Rows 9>38	Names of staff receiving documents – this list is in the order invoiced

Index

Chartered Institute of Library and Information Professionals (CILIP) 72

Chartered Institute of Management Accountants 74

Chartered Institute of Public Finance and Accountancy 74

Clements, D. W. G. 43

commercial libraries, purchase of periodicals 28

Companies House 50, 60

computer systems, design of 44

Corrall, S. 7

corporate reporting 58–60, *59*

cost accounting 41–42, 50–51

cost analysis 42–48

      drawbacks in library/information units 38

cost centres:

      budget development and *24*

      consolidation of data to 45–46

      'decision packages', as 22

      fund analysis 58

      identification of 43

      information units, as 10

      totals 60

      transactional listings 58, *59*

costing 38–48

      computer systems, design 44

      paperwork design 44